Providential

Providential

A Memoir of Growing Up, Education, and Learning to Be What We Are

THOMAS DEL PRETE

RESOURCE *Publications* • Eugene, Oregon

PROVIDENTIAL
A Memoir of Growing Up, Education, and Learning to Be What We Are

Resource Publications
An Imprint of Wipf and Stock Publishers
199 W. 8th Ave., Suite 3
Eugene, OR 97401

www.wipfandstock.com

PAPERBACK ISBN: 979-8-3852-7135-1
HARDCOVER ISBN: 979-8-3852-7136-8
EBOOK ISBN: 979-8-3852-7137-5

For Lena and Juliana

Contents

Preface

"Where do we come from? What are we? Where are we going?" are the three questions that Paul Gauguin famously used to frame one of his paintings, completed in 1897 and now on display at the Museum of Fine Arts in Boston. Like many of us would, as a young child I might have answered these questions in matter-of-fact and concrete terms—"We come from Providence, Rhode Island, we are the Del Prete family, and we are going to [insert one of several typical places, such as St. Mary's Church or Roger Williams Park]." Emerging from childhood, I might have used my customary social lens, focusing on my family's immigrant roots and our ethnic and Catholic identity. Nearing young adulthood, I might have cast the answers in a more personal and vocational mold, pointing to my sense of direction in the field of education. As a young adult, I might have thought about our progress as a society in realizing our democratic ideals; or I might have accepted the invitation to reflect in more existential and spiritual terms on what our lives as humans are all about, drawing on my Catholic religious upbringing and, once I finally met him through his writings, people such as Thomas Merton from whom I learned. These different ways of answering Gauguin's questions are all reflected in these pages; they all are part of the story of my journey from child to young adult and of my education and effort to determine my path and how I would try to live and work. Perhaps my story will encourage you to think about your own life journey with the same questions in mind.

Acknowledgments

This memoir germinated from a seed planted by Marv Hoffman, educator, writer, and friend, who posts a weekly reflection on his blog about his own life experience. My wife Elena and daughter Juliana offered valuable feedback and honest and loving encouragement as it formed. Of course, it would not exist at all if not for the influence of the beloved people who were part of my upbringing and education, in particular my mom and dad, my siblings Rob, Kathy, and Joe, and my teachers, mentors, and friends, all of whom are implicated in these pages.

1

Me, My Milieu, and Providence

> Now I become myself. It's taken
> Time, many years and places
>
> —May Sarton

We don't choose to be born or when or where. My location happened to be Providence, Rhode Island, my time in the middle of the twentieth century. If I had had a choice, I might not have used it to become part of the baby boomer generation. Fired up by books from the public library on Elmwood Street, my imagination roamed through time and space and possibility.

As a boy I romanticized the American Revolution, reading books like *Johnny Tremain* and wondering what role I would have played. For a while I wished nothing more than to explore the wilderness with Daniel Boone. In fact, one Christmas my parents gave me a fake coonskin cap and a miniature plastic flintlock rifle to indulge my devotion to the frontiersman, who was more rugged in my mind than the highly sanitized image presented by Fess Parker and his neatly fringed buckskins on TV. To my delight they were waiting for me under the artificial white Christmas tree decorated with the small blue matte bulbs, right next to the brown-stained wooden creche that looked like a three-sided log cabin made by Uncle Armand.

I still wish I could hang around with Benjamin Franklin for a while—any moment in a life so full of civic contribution, invention, sly humor, and wisdom would work for me. I would love to have listened to Abraham Lincoln in person, perhaps to his House Divided speech or his Cooper Union speech, in which he exhorts his listeners: "Let us have faith that right makes might, and in that faith, let us, to the end, dare to do our duty as we understand it." Regarding the latter one listener marveled at Lincoln's "face lighted up as with an inward fire; the whole man was transfigured"—how great it would have been to see him so animated by carefully reasoned conviction! Or to have listened to Frederick Douglass delivering his thunderous oration challenging the meaning of the Fourth of July.

In my imaginary wanderings and musings, I of course was influenced by the historical perspective afforded me today and perhaps also, despite my continuing study of it, historical naivete. I wonder what political positions and actions I would have taken and what my life would have been like during those momentous times in the eighteenth and nineteenth centuries without the benefit of the understanding I have now. So I must ask myself whether I've fully appreciated my own time and place and what it has meant to my own growth as a person.

Looking back, it's clear that my seventy years have coincided with an incredibly interesting time in American and human history, replete with its share of tumultuous and transformative moments. I was a growing boy during the Civil Rights movement in the 1960s and a newly minted teenager in 1968 when Martin Luther King Jr. and then Robert Kennedy were assassinated. Thomas Merton died accidentally that same year, someone whose spiritual and social writings I would later find so instructive, and whom I would come to know better through people who knew him personally. When Cassius Clay became Muhammad Ali, it registered, although in 1967 I didn't understand the significance of his principled objection to the Vietnam War and to being drafted to fight in it, and the boxing title it cost him. In my first year in college, in the fall of 1972, I wrote a long account of the issues involved in the case of Daniel Ellsberg and the *Pentagon Papers*, the classified report on the Vietnam War that Ellsberg felt compelled to disclose to the *New York Times* and *Washington Post* despite the risk of incarceration, a case still being adjudicated as I labored to capture it. Then there was President Nixon's resignation in the aftermath of the Watergate scandal involving his administration's break-in at the Democratic National Committee Headquarters, which opened my eyes forever to the difference between public service and politics. Scores by the composer John Williams captivated me a couple of years later; with everyone else I held my breath listening to the menacing notes signaling the impending arrival of the shark in the movie "Jaws" and then felt my spirit rise expectantly as notes of youthful courage played to open the first "Star Wars" movie.

I wish I could have taken an inquisitive stroll along the Maine seashore with Rachel Carson. I consider her one of those people from whom we all need to learn, worthy of emulation, someone who didn't simply go through life but felt and lived it deeply. She understood the ecology of the planet not only because of her inquiring and orderly scientific mind, but also because she had her hand on its living pulse in the nooks and crannies of the Maine coastline and elsewhere and stood in wonder at it, capturing it in language that wove poetically through her prose in books like *The Sea Around Us* and *The Edge of the Sea*. Like so many others I lived in the legacy of *Silent Spring*—her resounding alarm awakening us to the harm we collectively inflict on our ecosystem and ourselves. As a Boy Scout I participated in the first Earth Days, collected newspapers for recycling, and was even in a photo in the local paper with the mayor highlighting our troop's effort to "Save Our American Resources." We were strengthened in our resolve by a striking image—the "earthrise" photo taken by astronauts in 1968 as their Apollo 8 spacecraft orbited the moon. It depicts a partial globe of thick white swirls enfolding shades of blue and a patch of light brown suspended against a vast dark expanse, stunning us into awareness of a more beautiful and fragile and solitary home than we had imagined. It's the current screensaver on my phone.

Even as the Civil Rights and environmental movements seeped into my dim but growing social consciousness, the world of sports awakened my love of athletic movement and innate capacity for partisan loyalty. When I was around ten years old my dad took me and my brother Rob to watch Bill Russell play at the Boston Garden. We had seats behind one of the baskets as the Celtics legend battled Wilt Chamberlain and the Philadelphia 76ers. I was in awe of the two hoop titans tugging and pulling and pushing to get a positional advantage in the paint. I also was impressed by the breadth of Wayne Embry—it seemed to take me a full ten seconds to walk past him along one of the sidelines during halftime. Only later did I learn how Russell, the first Black coach in the National Basketball Association, stood tall not only on the court, but also for civil rights, standing alongside King and Ali and his Boston neighbors, among others, despite being threatened and his home violated for his public stance.

I shifted my baseball loyalty from Mickey Mantle and the Yankees to the Red Sox during their "Impossible Dream" season of 1967; I can recite for you Yaz's triple crown stats from that year. Decades later I celebrated with my then twelve-year-old daughter Juliana when the Sox "reversed the curse" of eighty-six years and won the World Series, fulfilling the hopes of fans in New England and beyond passed down through generations (the "curse" was widely believed to stem from the mind-boggling trade of the pitcher and slugger Babe Ruth to the Yankees before the 1920 season).

I kept a sports scrapbook for a time, one newspaper clipping noting Princeton hoop star Bill Bradley's stellar play against my hometown Providence College Friars, another a headline trumpeting the Friar's Jimmy Walker's fifty points against Boston College. Around the time that Bradley finished his studies as a Rhodes Scholar and started his decade of professional play with the New York Knicks, I read John McPhee's account of his incredibly disciplined approach to honing his game, *A Sense of Where You Are*. I took the book title to mean not only on the court but also in life; even as a young man Bradley seemed to know where he was in both.

When I started as an altar boy at St. Mary's Church in Providence, I learned the liturgical prayers and responses in Latin. But soon after, the reforms instituted by the Vatican II Council launched by Pope John XXIII (now Saint John XXIII) began to take hold. The transformation was palpable. The language of the liturgy was converted to English and the priest celebrating the Mass faced the congregation (so cool that priests were "celebrants"). The Mass became more accessible, participatory, and communal; it became *warmer*, with new roles for the laity, although more for men than for women.

As a boy I watched with my big-band-era and swing-music-loving parents as the Beatles made their debut on the Ed Sullivan Show, enamored with their sound but mystified by the frenzied fans swooning at their feet. When Neil Armstrong set foot on the moon in the grainy image that somehow beamed through our black and white Zenith TV, I contemplated in wonder his declaration of "one small step for man, one giant leap for mankind." I earned Space Exploration merit badge soon after, building a model Saturn V rocket and dreaming—with no sense at all of what would prepare me—of becoming an astronaut on an Apollo mission. As a veteran staff member at Camp Yawgoog I celebrated the U.S. bicentennial, donning a three-cornered hat along with my friend Hop in the staff photo, headgear that we brought back from a history road trip that included Williamsburg,

Virginia. I saw the Berlin wall fall on TV. I learned wonderingly about glasnost and perestroika in the Soviet Union under Gorbachev, and then about the dissolution of the U.S.S.R., hoping that it signaled not only the end of the Cold War but the beginning of the end of the threat of nuclear holocaust, which has lurked like a menacing apocalyptic figure throughout my conscious life. I could not have imagined then that I would marry someone with firsthand experience of life in the U.S.S.R., its breakup, and the anxiety and want spawned by its messy aftermath in the former Soviet states. In 2001 I watched soberly in real time with colleagues on the morning of 9/11 as one of the planes hit the twin towers in New York City, images that stunned us all into a silent realization that the world had suddenly turned upside down; everyone had the same impulse—to go home and make sure everyone they loved was safe.

Technology has taken such tremendous leaps during my lifetime, its impact so deeply woven into the daily lives of most of us on the planet, that it is hard to imagine a more transformative period, even for my grandparents born in the nineteenth century and living well into the twentieth. I can trace one strand of progress right at my desk. I wrote a couple of my undergraduate papers by hand, gradually becoming more proficient on the typewriter with my clumsy two-finger method. My improved digital dexterity relieved my mom, whose fingers thrummed on the keyboard, of the need to help me (I was a commuter living at home). It also compelled me to review carefully each sentence in my written scrawl and to concentrate intently to avoid the frustration of trying to erase or "white out" a mistake, smudging the typescript in the process; or worse, of ripping out the typing paper, crunching it into a ball to add to the pile at my feet, and starting again, a rejection made all the more irritating when I was using carbon paper to preserve a copy of my work. In the mid-1980s I completed my dissertation on an electronic word processor as well as a simple computer, using floppy disks. Within weeks I jettisoned the electronic word processor—it had become obsolete so quickly.

Now I live with a mixture of awe and concern at the computing power of our hand-held phones, global positioning technology, humanoid robots, and the growth of nanotechnology and artificial intelligence. In these feelings I am not unique, joining a historical chorus represented well by Henry Adams, historian and great-grandson and grandson, respectively, of the second and sixth presidents of the United States. While at the world's fair in Paris in 1900, Adams toured "The Hall of Electrical Machines" and encountered the technology that was in the process of transforming his era, epitomized by a large and mysteriously noiseless dynamo, a new and powerful source of energy. Impressed, he also worried that the cosmos was tilting off its base, contrasting the masculine force of the dynamo with the feminine and spiritual force of the Virgin that had powered art for centuries. We live with similar questions. When does awe of technology become worship and worship make us subservient? When does technology begin to erode the sensibilities and capacities that make us human? What are the deepest sources of human sensibility and understanding that we need to keep alive and well? I often feel a similar emotional pendulum when I consider the state of human affairs, who manages them and how technology influences them, and the question of why we are where we are. I wonder whether we can achieve a truly human-centered approach to our collective lives, to what extent we all can learn to cherish each other and our earthly home.

FROM FAMILIAR TO STRANGE AND BACK AGAIN

Of course, as much as my consciousness of the world has been shaped by the events of my time and the history that molded them, my life has been influenced by the personal and immediate—by my family and my geographical, educational, and cultural environment. My parents and grandparents have their own interesting histories, in many ways emblematic of the immigrant stories that have woven together so much of our social history in America. I am the eldest of four, with Rob, Kathy, and Joe following me in the short space of six years. In Providence we were surrounded by grandparents, aunts, uncles, and cousins, creating a kind of family cocoon in which to grow up. This was not unusual in an immigrant city such as Providence. Nor was our great family dispersal unusual: one-by-one we all moved from our multi-family homes to single-family homes to fulfill middle-class aspirations.

During our last months in our two-family home on Waverly Street—on the western side that slopes towards Route 10 just enough to propel us on our sleds when the sidewalks were icy—we would often take Sunday drives to look at houses listed for sale in the *Providence Journal* or to size up prospective neighborhoods. These trips supplanted family visits and our occasional jaunts to Roger Williams Park or the Rocky Point amusement park. I felt my curiosity regarding various ranch and colonial houses no match for the gravitational pull of Waverly Street and the intimacy of our neighborhood life. It never occurred to me that one day we might be separated from our older cousins living upstairs or from my maternal grandmother residing on the ground floor next door or, for that matter, my grandfather and cousins living within shouting distance on the corner of Ellery and Rosedale, right next to Ellery Street Park. Our cousin Nancy, our frequent and cherished babysitter, held a sweet-sixteen party around this time, in the basement of our house where her older brother's electric train set buzzed around on a green table next to a stand-up radio with a large mysterious dial from another age. But I never associated this party with the growth of a young woman who would be drawn increasingly to activity outside our family sphere. And I savored Grandma Degnan's apple pies and "poor man's bread"—how could that change? I simply did not apprehend the seriousness of my parents' quest until we packed things up to move a few miles away to North Providence. To borrow a lament from the poet John Donne, all coherence was gone.

But if there was loss there also was some continuity and considerable gain, and I can't imagine now changing the course that moving set for our lives. For one thing, except for one year, my education would continue a short distance down the road in the heart of Providence, right through my master's degree. For another, there was a wooded area behind our new home. It was small, protected as part of the town's water system, but I imagined wilderness adventures and tree houses. We did manage to build a couple of tree houses with help from new friends, and the woods were fun to explore, but outdoor adventure would arrive more expansively through an unexpected opportunity to join a new Boy Scout troop forming in our neighborhood.

After we finished our year of kindergarten at Althea Street School in Providence, located just a couple of crosswalks and one crossing guard from where we lived on Waverly, my parents enrolled me, then Rob, and then Kathy in parochial school. Moving interrupted this pattern. While I made it through 7th grade at St. Mary's Elementary School, affiliated with St. Mary's Church on Broadway, Joe never crossed the school's threshold (if pressed, Rob and I might say that the school was spared). In fact, Joe had to "drop out" of kindergarten at Althea Street, one of his dubious distinctions that his siblings are fond of recalling. Rob and I went to La Salle Academy in Providence for high school, at the time an all-boy's school run by the Christian Brothers, with my class of 1972 the hundredth overall. Girls were admitted to La Salle a decade or so after Rob graduated a couple of years after me. Kathy didn't enjoy her small all-girls parochial school and transferred to North Providence High School after pleading ("insisting" might be more accurate) with Mom and Dad. She must have had a premonition that she would meet her future sweetheart and husband Frankie Anzeveno there, and that his sports bona fides (including his impressive collection of Red Sox memorabilia) would endear him to her brothers.

Even as parental direction determined the course of our early lives, our own interests and inclinations slowly emerged and, for me, so did my awareness of my own internal compass. By compass, I don't simply mean my conscience, although that has been ever-present and active, due in no small degree to my Catholic upbringing, I am sure. I mean something more—what I can best characterize as my inner integrity, the whole me at my existential core. Learning to understand and live my own integrity has been a continuous part of my journey. This has not always been a conscious process, but more an intuitive one that I learned to accept as a central part of the experience of being me. In this I believe I have common ground with most people. Aren't we all in our own way trying to discover and live who we are; trying to live who we are fully, humbly yet unreservedly, even boldly; trying to live what some people, perhaps echoing Abraham Lincoln's appeal to the "the better angels of our nature," often refer to as our best self? And, starting with our parents or guardians, don't we look to others—need others—to help us, to affirm us and our effort?

PROVIDENCE AND INEXPLICABLE CARE

As a place to start growing into your full self, Providence offers a special reason for hope, if you consider the deeper meaning of the city's name. Roger Williams, the broad-minded minister condemned by Puritan authorities in Massachusetts for advocating, among other things, for the decoupling of church and state, is responsible for the city's name. He made the designation after escaping through dense woods in the winter of 1636 and negotiating for the land with Canonicus and his nephew Miantonomo, two sachems of the Narragansett people. Williams was a safe bet to complete a difficult winter trek. A man of conviction and resolve, in 1672, at about age seventy, my age as I write this, he rowed the entire length of Narragansett Bay, about a twenty-mile full-day journey from Providence to Newport, to engage in a theological debate with a group of Quakers on the question of a divine "inner light." In 1636 he was grateful for divine providence—for the divine guidance and care that brought him through his ordeal safely—and so Providence was born and became a haven for others.

You might be surprised to learn of Roger Williams's respectful negotiation with the indigenous people. A cynical view might point to economic motivation, and for sure there was opportunity: Williams offered to trade English goods with the Narragansetts in exchange. But the Narragansetts valued this exchange and furthermore saw Williams as a friendly potential buffer in ongoing territorial disputes involving the environs of Narragansett Bay with the neighboring Wampanoags, led by Ousamequin (the English knew him by his title, "Massasoit," which means "Great Sachem"). Also, unlike most of his English contemporaries, Williams's respect was more than transactional and expedient. He showed an anthropological interest in knowing his neighbors on their own terms, wondering also whether they had any connection to the Biblical lost tribes of Israel, leading to his *A Key into the Language of America*, a study of the Narragansett language and culture, the first of its kind in English.

Knowing the Providence backstory makes you think that your own journey will somehow work out. Mine included a love affair with books and sports and the buoyant life and community of a camp staff; led me deeply into the world of education as both student and teacher, motivated by a thirst for learning and the promise education holds for all of us. It also led me into the world of Thomas Merton, a monk with a lot to say about growing up and the inner life, feeding my propensity, for better or worse, to meditate on matters big and small, and nudging my occasional flirtation with the idea of the priesthood, not to mention monkhood. In fact, apart from my family, these three basic worlds of learning—school and intellectual, outdoor and experiential, religious and spiritual—played a powerful interactive role in my growth.

Providence has been with me throughout, in the web of people, choices, and opportunity in my life, and in accompanying and inexplicable forms of care and grace. But this is far from saying that I always understood where I was going or that I was on a clear linear path. Like Roger Williams, I've traveled through some wilderness moments in life and emerged with gratitude. I suppose like him I've also paid attention to my inner compass, guided forward by a moral sense and determination I did not always understand, manifested in my thirst to read and to learn, and a desire to do well and do right for myself and for my immediate and the broader world.

Especially in my adult life, it has led me more consciously not only to learn better how to be, but to ponder what being and being me and being you mean in a universe whose vastness and mystery astound—to learn, in Merton's words, "what we are" and so what I am in my humanity; to ponder how we learn to dance to the pulse of life around us and in us; to ponder how we attune to and harness our greatest power, the power of love.

I can say that the more I've learned of the history of my family, community, and the wider world the more I've become fascinated by it and wondered about it. They make up the social and cultural milieu woven into my life and are part of my education, too. I appreciate that I was born in the United States. I'm grateful for my forebears, especially my immigrant grandparents (paternal) and great uncles and aunts whom I knew firsthand, who made my American identity possible by uprooting their families and their lives to get here and start anew. I appreciate the primary communities in which I have lived, their diversity, vitalities, challenges, and the people who strive to thrive in them. I didn't know of course that I would make it to seventy years old; but here I am. I guess I shouldn't be surprised since my dad was with us until ninety-eight, and I was able to tell him that I was writing this; I'm not sure he understood the concept but felt his unfailing love and support as always. But we lost our mom much earlier, and you never know.

Writing is a way to remember and share and reflect on some of the formative, fortuitous, and funny (both humorous and curious) experiences of my growing up, and the places and people involved; and so, too, the providential ones. Writing also is a way to share and reflect on becoming who I am, on my formative experience and education, and on their larger meaning.

On its face my story is simple, and some aspects might be familiar. It's about a boy, the oldest of four siblings, not as tall physically as he wanted to be once he discovered basketball, a parochial school student with a penchant for learning, an avid reader; a boy who felt comfortable in a landscape of two- and three-decker houses in a predominately ethnic neighborhood with relatives all around and momentarily strange when his family moved to a neighborhood of single-family homes; a boy acutely attuned to his dad's sharp summoning whistle as he played within the radius of a block in his Providence neighborhood with his siblings and cousins and friends, and to the smell of fresh sauce made by his mom; a boy who thrived at camp but was shy with girls; a boy interested in understanding life while trying to live it well and convinced teaching was a way to change the world; a boy who experienced some of the complications and felicities of life along his particular way.

2

Childhood

There is no Frigate like a Book
To take us Lands away
Nor any Coursers like a Page
Of prancing Poetry—
This Traverse may the poorest take
Without oppress of Toll—
How frugal is the Chariot
That bears the Human Soul—

—Emily Dickinson

WHEN THE BIG WORLD CAME CRASHING INTO MY LITTLE ONE

As much as the unknown and unexpected are frequent companions in childhood, and you try to make sense of them, nothing could prepare me for the jolt that propelled the churn in my eight-year-old legs as I left St. Mary's Elementary at a run one Friday afternoon before Thanksgiving. The alarming message delivered over the school intercom that the president had been shot rattled in my brain. We were dismissed early, an abrupt disruption of routine. My instinct was to go where life felt safe, to go home as fast as I could.

So there I was rushing down Barton Street with my little blue tie with the "SMS" ("St. Mary's School") patch, impatient for the light to change so that I could cross Westminster and get to Messer Street and take a right on Hudson and book it down Ellery past Chapin Avenue where Mike DeLuca lived, past the park on the right between Wendell and Rosedale and then the home on the corner of Rosedale where my paternal grandfather and my Uncle Pete's family lived, before taking a right on Waverly, crossing in front of Eddie's house with the high bushes and then Kenny's and his fenced-in yard, and scooting through our alleyway to the back door to seek solace with Mom. It was a blurry three-quarters of a mile.

I knew the route by heart, walking to and from school most days, sometimes with my cousin Billy and later my brother Rob and sister Kathy, accompanied by rows of three-decker houses, their front porches opening to the streets, including on Wood Street where my parents grew up and met. There were familiar landmarks like the Table Talk Pie building on Westminster and the tailor shop on Messer whose entryway steps for some reason descended from the sidewalk, inviting you to peer in. Good thing Kathy knew the route, too, because she had to walk it alone one day in first grade when her oldest brother failed to meet her.

Once close to Waverly I was on my home ground and in the tightly woven social web of my extended family. Residing upstairs were my Uncle Vinny and Auntie Helen and four cousins—Johnny, Nancy, Barbara, and Billy—as well as Rusty, their frisky cocker spaniel. Older than me, my cousins sometimes played 45 rpm records by performers like Chubby Checker loud enough so that I could hear, the pulsating and electrifying beats much different from old melodies like "Daisy, Daisy, give me your answer do" that we sometimes sang around the house; so different from the big band and swing sounds emanating from the large boxy "hi-fi" record player Mom bought for Dad, the music that my parents loved to dance to. They fortuitously introduced me to "The Twist" and rock 'n' roll. From our backyard we could see the three-decker house in which my Uncle Pete's and Auntie Peggy's family and my paternal grandparents lived. My mom's mom lived next door on the first floor, where she produced the most delicious apple pies, along with Grandpa Degnan and Auntie Betty. My mom's Auntie Puggy (my great-aunt) and her cousin Irene lived upstairs.

My Dad's mother, whom we called "Nonnie," is a blurry figure in my memory; but her solicitous demeanor is firmly imprinted. We occasionally walked around the corner to her house for Sunday dinner, climbing the stairs to the third floor into aromas of provolone and sauce and pasta, expecting to be squeezed and exclaimed over, and hoping that she would usher us secretly into her pantry where she had a small stash of Hershey's kisses. The smells were familiar also because Mom produced them regularly in our home, an important benefit, from our point of view, of the tutelage she received while she and Dad lived in the same home as Dad's parents during their first year of marriage, one of Dad's brothers and his sister and their families on the first and second floors. This occurred years before any of us arrived, and Mom might have added that we reaped the benefit while she paid the cost living in a crowded home without knowing how to speak Italian. Nonnie would succumb to cancer when I was barely school age; I remember her swaddled in blankets and silence in a cushioned chair, in the living room where white doilies sat atop tables and where there was a piano that my Uncle Joe, the most unassuming of Dad's four siblings, had learned to play.

Nonnie's family were Sabatinis from Piedimonte San Germano, a village in Italy north of Naples in the vicinity of the Abbey of Montecassino. They were shepherded to Providence by my remarkable great-grandmother Theresa, whom my father would describe in awestruck tones as a "human dynamo." The family came in two shifts sandwiched around World War I, until all nine siblings and my great-grandfather Pietro were together. Elsie (Ersilia), the oldest child at age 23 and my grandmother, helped pave the way in the first shift in 1913. She and her sister Marietta apparently found work as seamstresses in a garment factory while their brother Ralph started barbering. Their youngest sibling was Luigi, known to my father and all of us as "Uncle Gene." Uncle Gene, by then thirteen years old, arrived in 1923 via Ellis Island in New York City, along with two of his older brothers and their older sisters who cared for them—my Great-Aunt Lena and her sister Dinda (Clotilda), makers of delectable egg and wine biscuits. He exemplified the best of the Sabatini personality—youthful, gregarious, and full of heart and life. If you were carrying around any anxiety, it was sure to dissolve in Uncle Gene's warm presence. He also embodied the Sabatini physical stature, which invariably made me think of Hobbits.

The neighborhood was our playground, and the parameters of our playing area were defined by the sound of my father's whistle. This was not as restrictive as you might think, because the familiar shrill carried about a block in every direction. Dad's whistle was distinctive enough that we would recognize it anywhere. It was a summons: when we heard it, we knew it was time to hustle home, usually for dinner. In his mid-nineties Dad responded willingly when my brothers and I asked him if he could still produce it. He put two fingers to his lips and it blasted out, striking a deeply resonant chord in us.

The street was as important a play space as any other, whether for hitting a ball about the size of a small beach ball and scurrying from a sewer cap to a telephone pole in our version of baseball or chucking a football while avoiding telephone lines. We rode bikes and roller skated on the sidewalks, unless we were trying to make rolls of "caps" pop while pounding them with a rock or trying to shoot through the duds with a cap gun. Ellery Street Park—before it was developed as a playground with the monkey bars that took out part of my brother Rob's front teeth, leaving a triangular gap, and a merry-go-round encircled by a small gulley produced by kids pushing it into a frenzied ride, which morphed into a narrow moat after it rained, and a wondrous array of baskets for hoops—was an uneven field in which we sometimes played tackle football. If you tilted up our makeshift playing area about twenty-five or thirty degrees, then you would have a mogul run fit for the Olympics; a kid could easily get lost for a moment behind a grassy bump or after a rolling pile-up and miss a play or two. The alternative was to go down to the end of Waverly just before the service road, on the right-hand side where we lived, and pick up some scrapes and bruises on the weedy and gravely lot near Bobby Tobin's house.

Days after JFK was assassinated, I was sitting on the floor in front of our black-and-white TV, Dad on a chair to my right, watching as a horse-drawn carriage with a flag-draped casket led the cortège for the president. Young Caroline and little John, the president's children, appeared near their mom, who was veiled in grief. I wondered how they felt.

My Dad, a social studies teacher with keen historical and political awareness and a Kennedy supporter, watched intently. Having lived through the Depression and World War II, he understood how the world can get unhinged, how large and largely invisible forces can affect ordinary lives. This was my first big intimation that our lives could be affected by something over which we had no immediate control, that we were part of a political system, that we couldn't take our lives for granted.

UNSETTLING MOMENTS IN SCHOOL AND THE NEIGHBORHOOD

Up to this point most of the aberrant or unsettling events in my life were on a much smaller scale. When I learned in 1961 that Mom was having another baby, I was sure that it would be a girl—that would give our family two boys and two girls, just like my cousins had upstairs. This symmetry seemed so foreordained that I was baffled when Mom arrived with Joe. I liberally expressed my need to rail at the injustice.

Then there was the startling incident in first grade. Mother St. G., young even to my young eyes, and cherubic in appearance despite the press of her pointed black and white habit against her cheeks and forehead, threatened to wash out the mouth of one of my classmates with soap and then proceeded one day to do exactly that. She held the malefactor near the sink behind the curtain, which fell to one side while the punishment was administered as promised. At least it was easy for me and the rest of us to believe so. We didn't see any telltale bubbles emerging from his mouth or nostrils, and we didn't dare rush up to check as more reckless first graders might have done. But we really didn't need to. Even if the chastening was Mother St. G's idea of instructive theater, it was a grim event, and we were convinced.

Even more dramatic, I found myself escorted into an ambulance one day from the school playground—the stretch of asphalt between the old three-story brick building housing St. Mary's of the Visitation school and Barton Street. There I had been innocently sharing what I thought was my mastery of the art of tripping with a fellow first grader. A key feature of my artistic rendering was to plant my right leg behind the left leg of my reluctant collaborator. Motivated by a strong sense of self-preservation, the left leg in question offered stiffer resistance than I anticipated, however, and to my utter disbelief and mortification, I lost my balance, falling backward. At that precise moment a robust third grader rumbled by, focused intently on a mission of his own. My head and his right foot met at the same time and in the same place on the ground.

The first nun to inspect the damage threw up her hands in a panic and ran off. Another nun arrived with a towel that she pressed onto the back of my head. There was an unnatural pause in the normal playground cacophony as the ambulance arrived. I remember being curious about this new experience, even though I was wobbly and had difficulty processing that the ambulance was there for me. My next vivid memory was of my concerned parents at my bedside at the hospital, ready to take me home after I had received ten stitches to close the wound on the back of my head. The scar remains, more visible now in the absence of camouflaging hair.

The boy whose foot had such an untimely encounter with my cranium felt bad about it. He sought me out in the playground to apologize; but more importantly wanted to know, on behalf of his mom, how my mom had managed to get the blood out of my jacket (his mom was clearly anticipating the need for such knowledge). I couldn't penetrate this mystery any more than he could. But my pride in my mom's cleaning prowess swelled, making up a little for the pride I had lost in my nonsensical effort to prove my physical prowess.

If I was humbled by the dramatic proof of my fraudulence as a master of tripping in first grade, I was unnerved one day when I was handed what I remember as an assignment involving primary colors, with an underlined red zero staring back at me. Somehow, I had not matched or ordered the colors properly; either that or I was simply sloppy, with one color seeping into the area of another. There I was in the last seat of the first row nearest the door trying to wish the paper away and contemplating my academic decline.

Of all the moments I remember in first grade—including my first attempts to learn French and practice printing and writing cursive within the lines of the writing paper we were given, making sure that the lower-case letters stayed below the dotted line between the two solid ones—getting that zero for my coloring assignment stands out. It stimulated a powerful reflex that I didn't know I had—my academic pride was wounded. It was an early intimation of an academic ego that I would have to learn to manage, not in first grade certainly, but years later as I advanced in my education, especially in the form of internal pressure I felt more than I would admit, which was greater than any external force.

Funny the relationship that can develop between achievement and pride and self-doubt. Too often my head, heart, and emotional center were like an effort at counterpoint in music, trying to achieve harmony from competing melodies in the form of messages circulating in my mind: keep your expectations in perspective; you don't have to prove yourself, just act out of your fullest self; achievement is a by-product of honest effort; keep your focus on learning. The best antidote to this annoying inner swirl was to lose myself in what I was doing. But as much as I managed to tune it out, I never completely shook off this legacy of my schooling. I called it to mind sometimes when as an adult I was in the role of teacher educator and visiting classrooms, including first grade classrooms in which children were afraid to get something wrong, and so afraid to do precisely what is important in learning—to risk a thought, venture an idea, try something out, and look the possibility of failure in the eye without blinking.

Not all the memorable events of my youngest years occurred in relation to school. One time a loud blast sent a shock of vibrations through the house. I don't know how young I was, but I remember being so shaken that I curled into a ball like a hedgehog and rolled myself behind the couch in our living room. It turns out that there was a gas explosion in a house across the street, and fire and police cars collected outside our front window. Later a volunteer fireman in Cranston, my Uncle Vinny from upstairs was one of the first on the scene and helped evacuate the one or two people who were there at the time.

Then there was Angelina's strange and recurring nocturnal lament, which resounded in the bedroom that my brother Rob and I shared. We slept in the same bed in the room closest to the backyard, on the side facing Kenny Capuano's yard, as soon as we outgrew our cribs. As we advanced in our single digit years and fell irresistibly under the spell of basketball, playing together on the St. Mary's CYO (Catholic Youth Organization) squad, we discovered that Boston Celtics games were broadcast on the radio. We naturally contrived to smuggle Dad's radio into bed whenever we could to listen to Johnny Most's gravelly voice announcing the game and raving indignantly about preposterous fouls called by the refs. We were mesmerized but invariably fell asleep by the end of the first quarter—unless we were kept awake by the intrusion of Angelina's strong and eerie voice.

Angelina was an elderly woman who lived kitty-corner behind us, on the third floor in the house on Rosedale next to my uncle's. After dark, sometimes in the last hour or two of the day, she took to opening her backyard window, which faced towards us, leaning on the sill to wail into the still night in singsong Italian. This happened nightly for days at a time. From what we understood from snatches of adult conversation, she would spool out lament after lament regarding real or imagined slights, or denounce neighbors, including my uncle, for some kind of immoral activity. What we initially regarded as a strange curiosity, so tempting to mock, became at times unsettling, and finally plain sad. One day an ambulance and a police car pulled up to her house on Rosedale. Hearing the hubbub, I hopped the chain link fence that separated us from our backyard neighbor—a practice

I followed sparingly out of respect for the flower garden she nurtured as well as the disapproval of various adults in my life—and stared at the scene. I felt a twinge of shame at my curiosity, natural as it was, when I saw medics guiding an old woman with arms wrapped in what looked like a white straitjacket. Things happened to people of which I had little or no awareness or understanding.

In another instance, our neighborhood was caught in some kind of vindictive crossfire involving some of the shadowy underworld attached to the Patriarca name that reared its ugly head from time to time in Providence—for example, in 1966 when Willie Marfeo was shot up in a phone booth. Someone threw a Molotov cocktail in the doorway of the three-story house across and up the street from us, on the corner of Ellery, causing a fire. This conflagration came on the heels of a shot being fired late at night through one of the second-floor windows on the Ellery Street side. The house was on the path that took us to Jack's corner store on Althea Street, adjacent to Union Avenue, where we would go occasionally to get a cool twelve-ounce glass bottle of RC Cola after playing on a hot day; you would have to walk by on the Waverly Street side and then turn right to cross in front of the house on Ellery. We gawked at the charred doorway and the bullet hole from a safe distance. But when Mom asked me to go alone to Jack's to get something she needed, I sprinted past both, unsure about what it all meant, feeling that it was like a menacing maelstrom that would suck me in if I got too close.

Sometime after I entered my double-digit years, I ventured beyond the immediate neighborhood to what I considered its outer reaches, going either to Olneyville or Cranston Street. If my parents didn't give me hearty encouragement, neither did they express concern; after all, I walked back and forth to school, and they knew I knew my way. My solitary jaunts were usually motivated by Christmas shopping. I reached Olneyville by taking the service road as far as it would go towards Westminster, my destination the Atlantic Mills Store situated between Manton Avenue and the Woonasquatucket River. I was familiar with Olneyville from its reputation for the best hot wieners around, and for servers who made six or so at a time, lining up the soft rolls right on their arms, filling them with wieners straight from the grill, and spooning and sprinkling on onions, mustard, and celery salt. But I knew Olneyville mainly because of the Olneyville Boys Club. I had been going there with my brother Rob since around six years old to learn to swim. Both Mom and Dad were good swimmers, Dad had been a lifeguard in his youth, and we went to Scarborough beach in the summers, so learning to swim was something that had to happen in the natural course of things.

Built in 1925, the year before Dad was born, the Club seemed on the far side of a timeline between new and old. Once there, we would jump out of our clothes, run naked through the showers, clutch ourselves to keep from shivering, and jump in the pool as soon as the lifeguard let us. Learning the dog paddle and leg kicking seemed straightforward and I thought my progress was good. But my swim test exposed the gap between my uncertainty and confidence. The problem was "the deep end" of the pool. We didn't practice there, and I guess it had assumed something like the status of a mythic monster in my mind—"*the deep end*." When I jumped into it for my test, I stopped swimming and started thinking, preoccupied with the notion of "deep" and thrashing around. I was like the suddenly self-conscious centipede in the rhyme who, when asked by a toad in fun which leg followed which, "worked his mind to such a pitch" that he "lay distracted in the ditch/considering how to run."

I was genuinely worried about this freeze in my momentum but was determined to thaw it out and qualify to jump off the diving board. Just as for most endeavors, I needed to be in the right state of mind; but I wasn't sure I could count on that. My solution: swim as fast as I could. On my second try sometime later, I swam blindly and earned my "S" (for "Swimmer"). To dwell or to plunge? Think or act? To hang on or let go? When is one overthinking or prudent, the other impulsive and foolish or liberating? These were the questions and they have stayed with me, pressing at times and in welcome moments free from thinking and full of being, not at all.

My alternative to Olneyville was to head in the opposite direction to go to Cranston Street. I was familiar with the A&P supermarket there, where Mom shopped and where we got the paper shopping bags that we measured and cut up to make covers for our schoolbooks at the beginning of every school year. We sometimes invaded a bakery there on Sundays after Mass for treats like chocolate-covered eclairs, picking up a loaf of Crugnale's Italian bread on the way. Crugnale's Italian bread was a family favorite at that time, with a flavorful blend of hard crust and soft inside that we relished. A loaf of Crugnale's didn't last long; between the moment we were seduced by the aroma and begging in the car for a hunk of an encrusted heel and the end of our Sunday noontime staple of pasta, salad and meatballs, it usually disappeared. On Cranston Street I would go to one or two of the small stores near the bakery and, on Mom's recommendation, look for a small bottle of Aqua Velva after-shave lotion for Dad.

READING, DAD, AND MY MYSTERIOUS DISAPPEARANCE FROM SECOND GRADE

The most unexpected event in my young school career occurred in second grade, where I made a brief appearance. Second grade might have been the only one taught by a lay teacher, a besweatered woman we knew as Ms. Gibbs. I remember little from the class, except the feeling of contentment while eating my breakfast of buttered toast after having served an early Mass while the other kids worked on math. Then one day, perhaps three weeks into the year, I was shepherded to an adjacent class through the door adjoining the two rooms. And suddenly I found myself in third grade with Mother St. Ann Linda and my cousin Billy who lived upstairs from me.

I wasn't against being in third grade. I simply was unsure how to respond. I did have some concern about knowing the times tables, but it turns out I was up to the task, one time reciting the three times table faster than anyone else in a speed competition, something I didn't know I could do; my attention to math workbooks that my father brought home—I'm not sure when I started with them but remember being nudged to do them by both Mom and Dad—had sharpened my arithmetic skill. Mom would sit by me occasionally, but her attention was taken up almost entirely by my younger siblings, all three of whom had arrived by the time I was crunching buttered toast one morning in second grade. Pungent cloth diapers boiled continuously, it seemed, in a large pot on the stove, and a milk bottle was always warming in a pot of water alongside the kettle whose hot water sometimes helped heat our baths. I would later learn that the school leadership in some form had met with my parents after Ms. Gibbs apparently said that there was not much she could teach me in second grade. Suffice it to say I was not conscious at the time of being beyond the scope of the second-grade curriculum. I knew only that I was always eager to engage in schoolwork.

Reading and writing were the core foundation of my academic acumen, with reading leading the way. Reading seemed as necessary as breathing to me, a process that I had internalized early enough that I don't remember much about learning it, except for my distaste for phonics in a couple of the workbooks my father brought home. All of us need to learn to enjoy words and trust our ability to get to know them, but we may need different ways to get to that point. All of us need steady exposure to the meaning and pleasure of words in poems and songs and stories that we like enough to want to hear them or read them again and again. I fed this need like I fed my body. What the Renaissance humanist scholar Erasmus said would have made as much sense to my younger self as it did when I encountered his words as an adult: "When I have a little money, I buy books; and if I have any left, I buy food and clothes." So would Emily Dickinson's poem proclaiming the power of books to bear our souls and take us lands away.

By the time I entered second grade I was a proficient reader eager to enter the lives and worlds books represented. This was due partly to the selection of books we had in the house at the time. Picture books, so wonderfully plentiful and available now, were much scarcer in those days, at least with us. My sister Kathy remembers *The Little Engine That Could* and I do, too; but not when it appeared. My dad was more familiar with traditional stories, and occasionally he brought home books in this vein for me to peruse from the state prison in Cranston, where in the 1960s he helped prepare inmates for the high school equivalency exam two or three early evenings a week. So I read *Robinson Crusoe*, *Treasure Island*, and *The Adventures of Tom Sawyer*. With his encouragement I gave *David Copperfield* a good try at an early age. Although I didn't understand this thick book fully, I was enamored nonetheless with young Copperfield, who himself learned to read with his aunt and uncle when he was about five or six, and how he survived the insufferable characters who tried to manipulate him for their own gain and overcame the difficulties that complicated his journey from boy to young man. It remains one of my favorite tales, and like *Adventures of Huckleberry Finn*, it is a book I've re-read with greater insight and appreciation as an adult. I've enjoyed also their enduring literary influence, especially in the form of Barbara Kingsolver's *Demon Copperhead* and Percival Everett's powerful retelling of Mark Twain's novel from the point of view of Jim, the enslaved man representing all of the enslaved, whose humanity he dignifies by granting him his full name (James, the title of the novel), voice, and intelligence.

The Scholastic Book Club was a great boost to my young reading life. Especially in fourth grade, I remember eagerly awaiting the arrival of the monthly book order form. All sorts of intriguing titles on the form, with short one- or two-sentence summaries, captured my imagination. A dollar or so might net me a couple of titles, like *The Black Stallion*, which Mother St. Theresa would hand out when they arrived. I kept most of them in the storage slot in my school desk, ready for when I finished my desk work early. I was all too aware that they were there waiting for me—it was as if they were alive and anxious for me to finish as much as I was. Mother St. Theresa, a slight figure seemingly lost in her all-encompassing black habit and steadfast in her commitment to teaching us English through sentence diagramming, apparently kept note of my avid reading habits. One day she gave me a folder filled with presidential biographical sketches, published in a series, that she had carefully cut out of a newspaper. She told me she thought I might like to read them. I was stymied somewhat by what I later realized was their scholarly language, historical allusions, and density, and struggled through some before setting them aside. What struck me most was the discovery of her faith in me and her intellectual side (an inner life I could never imagine then).

My best source of books was the library. I'm not sure when Dad first took me and brother Rob to the Elmwood branch. We usually drove, but I remember walking there once or twice—less than a mile but a good stretch—and coming home with a pile of books in my arms. Dad otherwise schooled us in language at home in the natural course of conversation. Funneling sensibilities sharpened by his Jesuit professors at Boston College (BC), he might encourage us to "enunciate" a word. At other times, he would introduce a word calculated both to expand our vocabulary and put us in our place, such as "I don't like your altitude," "You're too impetuous" (true!), or "You're being 'insolent' [really, Dad?], 'churlish,' or 'uncouth'" (for the record, my brothers Rob and Joe heard the latter somewhat more than I did; sister Kathy stayed mostly well above the need for this kind of verbal intervention, and we credit our occasional waywardness for strengthening her character).

It was probably in high school that I began to fully appreciate Dad's contribution to my vocabulary and enjoyment of words. Dad started teaching at La Salle Academy in 1950, getting the opportunity on the strength of his BC degree in history, which was sandwiched around his year in the army and sojourns in Guam and Saipan just after the war ended. In the early 1950s there seemed no limit to class size, Dad teaching history and English to thirty or more students at a time. He kept a thick, dense, and green-covered "Prose and Poetry" book in his bookcase at home that I think he used, and which I found daunting. I don't know how he managed it, especially during the few years when he hustled after school to Narragansett Brewery, located off Route 10 in Cranston, joining my Uncle Vinny for a shift there. For a while, he accomplished all of this without owning a car, often riding on the same bus as his students.

Dad landed a public-school teaching position at Aldrich Junior High in Warwick around the time I was born, ending his career thirty years later as the head of social studies at Winman Middle School. He stayed on at La Salle for a few years as the inaugural wrestling coach, recruited by Brother Anthony, who was still going strong as the athletic director when I arrived there. Dad was no stranger to sports. He received a football scholarship to go to BC, thanks to the advocacy of Al Morrow, a star player and the older brother of his friend Bill. He otherwise might not have gone to college at all; the youngest of five, the lives of my future uncles and aunt upended by World War II, he was the first and only one to go.

Dad played football at BC—primarily as a fleet "flanker" with good hands, sometimes playing "both ways" (offense and defense)—until he was drafted into the army towards the end of his first season, finishing his degree afterwards with support from the "GI Bill," which made college possible for so many of his generation. He had previously played football, run track, and competed in the high jump at Central High School in Providence. He also had a stint on the wrestling team at Central, but wrestling wasn't his forte. That didn't deter him. Somewhere he picked up a couple of wrestling books, including the guidebook produced by the U.S. Naval Academy, and applied what he learned, breaking things down "by the numbers," as he put it. He earned the respect of his La Salle team as well as La Salle's first state championship in 1960. Four and five years old respectively, my brother Rob and I attended a Saturday practice or two with Dad, giving Mom a break, and we still can name most of the champions, including Dennis Kearny (undefeated and unscored upon), Joe and John Cerra, Ray Palmisciano, and Norm Labutti. Norm reconnected with Dad when he relocated in his nineties from our long-time home in North Providence to an assisted living facility in Florida, still calling him "Coach."

One day, Dad was talking to me and opened his wallet. The topic of conversation had nothing to do with my sad pecuniary state, which depended on tips from the Sunday paper route that my brothers and I ran in the neighborhood, so I was curious. Dad pulled out a small, folded piece of red paper with a list of words and their definitions that he kept and handed it to me. To me, this was a real treasure, as much for what it said about Dad as a learner and teacher as for its intrinsic value. I kept it in my wallet for years until it basically disintegrated.

SIZE AND STATURE

My transition to life as a third grader progressed smoothly. Only over time did I become conscious that I was smaller than almost all my classmates, and that the girls seemed much older and more mature. In other words, as much as my intellectual and academic work kept pace, I was aware that the physical and social dimensions of my grade-level experiences were different than what they might have been. I was reminded of this from time to time. In 7th grade at St. Mary's, for example, I became more aware of a trio of girls in our class—Margaret Talacko, Susan Ricci, and Rosemary McBride—who were focused and studious and whose suppressed amusement regarding something or someone seemed to me sophisticated. Then there was my second year in public school (counting kindergarten), in eighth grade at Greystone Elementary in North Providence, where we had moved.

Greystone Elementary had been housed in a drooping box-like structure clothed in shingles that looked like coarse sandpaper on Waterman Avenue. So it was with great expectation one day in the early fall of 1967 that we grabbed our books and trudged up Woodcliff Avenue to the new one-level school building spread out along Morgan Avenue. Yes, our route traversed many avenues; but this will give you the wrong idea if you consider an avenue something grander than a street. They were just ordinary roads without any dividing lines, but for some reason the roads in our new neighborhood were mostly "avenues" or "drives"; in fact, our new home was on Barbara Ann Drive (presumably named in honor of the catchy if bleating tune with the same name by the Beach Boys).

Among my new classmates at Greystone was Audrey Fox. Audrey, who sat behind me, would poke me when the spirit moved her, smile when I turned around annoyed, and declare me "cute." This was not cute in the girl-boy sense, about which I vaguely understood Audrey to have a vast knowledge, but in the girl-toy-doll sense—I was that small to her. I wish she had considered that I started on the school basketball team, was one of two players to score at least twenty points in a single game, and helped represent the team in the town all-star contest. I should mention that the other twenty-point scorer was David Sorafine. Along with Mike McBride and Norman Jakeman, David was a fellow denizen of the short asphalt court with rusty metal backboards sitting along one edge of the closely packed array of mill homes in the Greystone area of North Providence; we often played two-on-two together. This court was like an oasis when I first discovered it through a path in the woods behind our new home, which was partly protected from development as part of the town water system. David also was at least six feet tall on his way to six feet, ten inches and Division III All-American play at then Bryant College.

But Audrey was gentle compared to Ralph Vitale. About twice my size when you consider height and breadth, Ralph thought it would be fun one day during recess to pick me up from behind and launch me skywards; but he overestimated his prowess, and in a split second I lay unconscious in the schoolyard, to the chagrin of our eighth-grade teacher, Mr. Shadoian. When Ralph, on the opposite team from mine in the town all-star game, came prancing up the court with a high dribble at about the level of my eyeballs, I was incredulous. As I moved in to defend him, I asked him what he was doing. He smiled, perhaps unconsciously seeking redemption for dropping me on my head. After a moment of hesitation, I did what I had to do and stole the ball.

As a freshman at La Salle Academy, a mere five-foot-two-inch, ninety-two-pound boy, I was among the last cut for the hoop team, and I was underweight for the lowest weight class in wrestling, which was ninety-eight pounds. I still thought I would grow into the sleek six-foot-two-inch athlete that I imagined (Dad, after all, was five-foot-eleven-and-a-half inches tall by his account); I just needed my growth spurt. Unfortunately, Dr. Taft, our pediatrician, hadn't offered any support for this vision to this point. A kindly man whom Mom clearly trusted, he otherwise never failed to offer a lollipop to reward our patience with his stethoscope and the probe he put in our ears. His alter ego was Dr. Fletcher, whom Mom took me to see when she noticed that my left leg was shorter than my right. Dr. Fletcher verified the discrepancy, but only after pressing a tape measure with a metal end into each of my hips without the least regard for my threshold for pain. There was some speculation that polio was the cause of my asymmetry (I remember ingesting the sugar cube containing the vaccine), but nothing came of it. Dr. Fletcher didn't support my vision of my future athletic self either, recommending that I wear a special heel on my left shoe to right my listing self and avoid appearing even shorter. I did, and it seemed weird; it also didn't seem to make any difference to my physical movement and so, thankfully, we eventually abandoned the idea of keeping my hips level.

My vertical growth gene never activated like it was supposed to, no doubt fought off by a competing Sabatini gene, and I ended up accepting a five-foot-eight-inch version of my ideal self, give or take, and shifting my attention to how high I could jump. For the most part I stopped noticing my smaller size relative to my classmates; it didn't seem to matter. Still, I have wondered about the impact of skipping a grade on my potential to play sports and my social life. I've discussed this question with my friend Marv Hoffman, who skipped a grade in middle school while growing up in Brooklyn during the 1940s and 50s; Marv, his height inversely proportional to his expansive mind and heart, has wondered the same. Marv is one of the most discerning and empathetic educators and humans I know. We agree that we would advise our younger selves to stay at grade level, provided that our schools would expand our curriculum opportunities within and beyond the classroom. This is more the norm today, setting aside extraordinary exceptions.

THE PERILS, PERKS, AND GLORIES OF BEING AN ALTAR BOY

I was also indelibly marked by what happened to my brother Rob in church one day, not least because of the shadow it cast on my own character. First, the background. For about a year I had been serving as an altar boy, having dutifully learned my pre-Vatican II Latin prayers and responses, and practiced ringing the bell to focus the attention of congregants on important moments during the Mass. I was trusted to light the candles on the altar without mishap. This task was more precarious than you might think. The altar was an imposing edifice for someone well shy of double digits in age, a veritable Goliath to my David in terms of proportion. To reach the candles I had to use a pole through which a wick was threaded on one side, opposite a cone-shaped candle snuffer on the other. I had to light the wick and stretch the pole towards each candle set in its golden holder. "Stretch" is the operative word, as it took all the length I could summon from my slight and short stature, leaning forward on tiptoes, to reach the wick of a candle. My effort at elongation was challenged to a greater or lesser degree depending on whether the candle was fresh and tall or melted down into stubbiness. If the Mass was a special celebration, then candle lighting was a more dramatic affair, as there were candelabra with seven candles each to illuminate. In my view, candelabra had a temperamental equilibrium—approach one with your wick or candle snuffer and they were apt to totter and sway like the masts of a ship caught in a driving tempest. It was hazardous work, and my parents held their breath when I had to undertake it before the Mass started, hoping I wouldn't set the altar cloths ablaze. Sometimes hot wax leaked onto the altar. My mom tended to avert her eyes.

At that time, probably the most critical task for an altar boy was to locate and hold the patten steady. The patten was basically a small golden plate with a handle. We altar boys had to place the patten under the chin of each communicant as they knelt to receive a consecrated host from the priest, a safeguard lest the communicant's tongue inadvertently withdraw as the priest endeavors to place a host on it, or the priest inadvertently fumbles the handoff, or something else untoward occurs, like an unexpected sneeze. An altar boy could be called on to save the day at any moment. We had to stay alert.

My brother Rob, younger than me by fourteen and a half months, was in the altar boy apprentice program. He was "an observer" and at the very beginning stage of his mastery of the patten. One Sunday I was the main altar server while Rob was taking his first turn as observer and patten-holder. Our parents must have been proud of our joint appearance on the altar.

Mass was being celebrated by Monsignor Mahoney. The monsignor, old from my perspective, was the embodiment of old-school. He didn't exactly breathe fire and brimstone, but he was unapologetic in using the fear of hell as a motivational tactic. He erred on the side of authoritarian paternalism and was impressively firm in his expectations concerning protocol. Suffice it to say he was more enforcer than educator.

When it came time for communion, the monsignor brought the chalice filled with consecrated hosts to the altar rail. Rob, still developing his altar boy reflexes, was a little slow getting to the altar rail with the patten, and I sensed a hint of impatience from the monsignor. But I was kneeling facing the altar, in the opposite direction of the altar rail. In those last days before the church reforms of post-Vatican II, everyone faced forward towards the altar during the Mass, including the priest.

Suddenly my attention was jerked towards the altar rail. Monsignor was berating Rob—apparently a host had eluded his vigilance and landed on the floor. He turned to me and said something to the effect that I should have been holding the patten and banished Rob to the side. I felt myself tighten, my response to somehow being held responsible while Rob was being publicly admonished.

I didn't at the time question the monsignor's manner and use of authority or his neglect of Rob's feelings—he didn't check with Rob afterwards to talk about what happened. Perhaps his gruff treatment reflected his view that adherence to form and ritual was the way to lead a soul to salvation. It led my soul to be wary of him. Rob decided that the life of an altar boy was too harsh for his taste.

The site of this indignity was St Mary's Church on Broadway in Providence, an impressive edifice built in a Gothic style with light gray granite quarried from the southwestern part of the state in 1869. Mom and Dad were married there in 1950, as handsome a couple as ever graced the arched doorway, as testified by photos and a grainy film of the joyous event. Both my parents grew up in the largely immigrant and Catholic neighborhood that made up the parish, about a half dozen blocks away on Wood Street. Dad fully Italian and Mom a mix of Irish and French-Canadian, their marriage reflected both the neighborhood and the church congregation. It also evoked mutterings from those not as sanguine about mixed ethnic alliances; but they were part of an accepted trend. Three of four of my father's siblings married a non-Italian and my mother's closest sister, Auntie Ginny, married my Uncle Louie.

St. Mary's Church was part of a small compound, with a large Victorian house alongside serving as a rectory for the resident clergy, and a stately burnt red brick building housing both St. Mary's Academy, a high school for girls, and the elementary school (the elementary school was transplanted in a new bland shoebox of a building about the time I was in sixth grade). When I entered my fifth-grade classroom for the first time in the old building, I was greeted warmly by Ms. Garvey, otherwise known for her stern demeanor. She recognized me right away, saying that my smile was just like my mother's, one of her many former students. From that moment I resolved to master fractions and be a model fifth-grader.

There were unexpected perks in being an altar boy while going to Catholic school with the sponsoring church next door. For one thing, you might be asked to serve at a funeral Mass. Apart from the privilege of missing school time, which gave you an enviable status among your peers, you might earn a token of gratitude from a bereaved family member in the form of cash. Usually this meant a dollar or two tucked in an envelope that was discreetly handed over at the end of the service. Occasionally the priest would be the bearer of this gratuity, having received a similar token himself.

Sometimes, you would be asked to serve Mass at 7:00 a.m. Early morning Mass had a devoted following. My Dad would go as much as he could during the penitential season of Lent before heading off to school to teach, and he and Mom went every day during Dad's retirement years that they shared together. The downside of serving early morning Mass for an altar boy like me was that you had to fast beforehand to heighten your spiritual hunger for the Lord and readiness to receive holy communion. This was not as big a trial as it sounds because you didn't skip breakfast, just delayed it. Not only that, but you got to eat breakfast at your desk in your classroom, provided your mom packed it for you, while everyone else stole secret and covetous glances your way. I was eager to check my brown paper lunch bag with breakfast included. I relished the simple breakfasts Mom prepared—usually slices of buttered toast with the buttered sides facing each other, cut in half and ready to be pulled apart and eaten one by one. Lunch was more robust—a sandwich made of liverwurst and cheese or ham and cheese or, if we were lucky, ham and provolone with roasted peppers or broccoli rabe, together with a piece of fruit. Occasionally, especially when I was older, I might find the heel of a loaf of Italian bread brimming with such satisfying fare; you could feel Mom's love and impeccable sense of what was good for you seeping through.

Soon after I turned ten years old one of the younger of the trio of Irish priests who served St. Mary's parish rewarded us altar boys with an invitation to go to a movie theater to see "The Sound of Music." It was 1965 and the movie had just opened. I was excited about this unusual opportunity, thoroughly enchanted when I heard Julie Andrews's angelic voice, and moved by how as a governess she used music to help the Trapp family children discover their true hearts and voices. I was sure that the heart of their dad would have to thaw in response and felt relief when it did, and greater relief when the family escaped from Nazi thralldom over the Alps. We hadn't gone to many movies as a family up to that point, with "Mary Poppins" the most memorable. We did watch movies on TV; I waited every year for the annual showing of The Wizard of Oz, never tiring of it. Mom was by far our best guide for movies. She seemed to know all the actors and actresses and films from the nineteen-thirties onward. She enjoyed different genres, drama and romance especially, but also, on occasion, horror, to my surprise given her gentle demeanor.

Being an altar boy also meant participating in the processions and pageantry of the traditional Catholic Church. You prepared for your role in the sacristy—the space hidden from view behind the altar where the vestments for the priests and altar boys were kept. Pageantry required special ceremonial garb. Instead of the plain black cassocks and white surpluses worn for ordinary services, we altar boys wore white cassocks and, depending on the occasion, either red or blue sashes and capes, with golden fringe on each. You wouldn't have been surprised if angels appeared trumpeting in approval.

There were various possible roles to play. You might lead one procession carrying a large cross and during another act as an acolyte and carry a large candle. Either of these roles could challenge your seven- or eight-year-old arm strength; the cross was about seven-foot-tall and I had visions of losing control of it to the detriment of nearby craniums. You might also carry the golden bucket of holy water, with its accompanying sprinkler, otherwise known as the "aspergillum." The sprinkler is a handle with a porous knob at one end that allows the priest to sprinkle holy water onto the gathered faithful. As an altar boy in the direct path of the priest's swinging arm, you were invariably showered many times, giving you added protection against sin in addition to a glistening holy aura.

But in the hierarchy of altar boy roles, for me carrying the censor stood tallest. The censor comprised a round or multisided base with an ornate cover dotted with small openings, the whole attached to several fine chains, two or so feet long, converging at a ring that acted as a handle. The priest spooned incense onto a round hot coal located in the base, transforming it into an aromatic vapor that drifted through the holes. As an altar boy, you had the immense responsibility of lighting the coal beforehand and otherwise holding the smoking censor level and steady or swinging it in a roughly forty-five-degree arc to create a cloud of incense. For a glorious moment you were an arbiter of intoxication.

THE SCHOOL PLAYGROUND, A QUASI-DUEL, AND PITCHING BASEBALL CARDS

We played a lot of games on the school asphalt, aka the playground, including "Red Rover" and tag. Red Rover could be physically jarring. Two lines of kids would face each other across the width of the playground. One by one we would call out each other's names—"red rover, red rover, [insert a kid's name] come over!" The callee would then gallop across the open space, choosing which pair of clasped hands to try to break through. If the hands held against the furious onslaught, then the runner was captured and added to the group. Invariably, however, the oncoming runner looked for a weak link in the human chain while we all braced ourselves. Of course, elementary kids come in all sizes and forms, with some as stout as tree trunks and others like the slenderest beginning of a future tree. I was of the latter variety—although most of my family members would contend that I have never left the slender stage—and remember having to brace myself with limited success numerous times. It didn't seem to matter all that much anyway. I don't remember any single side capturing all the members of the other side, although we sometimes had high-stakes moments when we would call lots of kids to come over. Recess may not have been long enough to finish the game, but Red Rover had intensity and drama and drained off a lot of boyish energy.

The playground was not always salutary. It was there—in the shadow of the church no less—that I first heard some of the slurs of that time, such as "fag" or "queer." I didn't know what they meant, and I suspect that most of the kids using them didn't either. But like me they understood the tone and derision of taunting, and they used language to retaliate against a slight or to goad or bully. I don't remember much if any fisticuffs, but I vividly remember a close call that I had.

It was like a scene from *The Three Musketeers*, only we didn't have swords, and we were seventh graders. I found myself after school facing Albert Berarducci from a relatively safe twenty or twenty-five feet, with a small group of intently curious kids looking on. Albert had said we would meet after school, and I felt that I had to be there or suffer the shame of cowardice. I had crossed some red line in Albert's world, and he had thrown down the gauntlet. It must have been something I said, but I wasn't sure. All I knew was that Albert, who had defiantly long hair and whispers of facial growth, and whose family ran a funeral home, an ominous sign, could easily be confused for an eighth grader and would likely pummel me. As you might suspect, I had one foot poised to run if things got tight; speed was the one asset I had.

Or so I thought. Alongside Albert stood Mario DeQuattro. Mario was a rugged guy in the mold of Jim Brown, the running back for the Cleveland Browns. In fact, he played that position and was the punter for La Salle Academy when we were both there. He looked like Albert's second in this duel, quadrupling the odds against solitary me; but it turns out he was sizing up the situation very thoughtfully and concluding that things weren't right. He seemed to restrain Albert and then to my surprise he asked him to stand down, announcing for the benefit of all present that nothing was going to happen. No one—least of all me—was about to question Mario in that moment or in any other for that matter. The tension dissolved, the kids dispersed, and I looked at Mario with great respect, feeling that he was a true instrument of God's mercy. Playground bullies are too numerous; playground gods are rare. Mario was a playground god.

Of all the playground activities, my favorite by far was pitching baseball cards. Pitching cards had a special allure: the challenge of accurate pitching, the prospect of winning cards, and the chance of adding to your collection of revered baseball heroes. Each small carboard card had an image of a baseball player in uniform on the front and the player's stats, year by year, in minute print on the back. They were a treasure trove of information for young fans, and you absorbed the data without trying. So many kids who struggled with math in school could recite batting averages or earned run averages of their favorite players and tell you how they were calculated. These days, drawing on what seems like an expanding universe of available statistics, kids can rattle off on-base percentages, slugging percentage, strikeout rate, and exit velocity. Like other kids, I had a stack of cards in my pocket, ready if called upon to verify a point or resolve an argument during the unceasing exchange of baseball information that dominated playground discourse even more than the taunts and assertions regarding character and capability that kids tossed carelessly about.

Baseball entered my consciousness at an early age. Like other Italian Americans, my dad was a Yankee fan, which is to say, he was a fan of Joe DiMaggio. Baseball is famous for its monikers and Joe had his share. He was known variously as "Joltin' Joe" (which you would know if you listened to Simon and Garfunkel's "Mrs. Robinson") or the Yankee Clipper and, by some, as the short-lived husband of Marilyn Monroe in the mid-1950s. People also knew who you were talking about if you simply said, "Joe D"; he was recognizable in this respect just as "Michael" in later years was all that was necessary to evoke the great hoop star Michael Jordan.

Among other notable accomplishments, Joe D. still holds the record for the longest hitting streak in baseball—fifty-six consecutive games or about a third of an entire baseball season—which he established in 1941. Hitting a baseball hurled at you with various spins and contortions from a mound sixty feet, six inches away might be the most difficult of all sports skills, although I think the challenge of scoring a goal in soccer rates consideration. I can't explain why the distance between pitcher and batter is measured thus, except to say that it was deemed optimal at some point to ensure the intense drama between the mound and the batter that occurs with every pitch; either that or, no matter how puzzling or obscure in origin, it is a sacred part of baseball heritage immune to interrogation. In any case, the durability of Joe D.'s hit record illustrates why it's hard for a professional baseball player to hit the ball at all, let alone bat .300; that is, get on base via a hit an average of at least one-and-two-tenths times out of every four. Joe D. had a lifetime average of .325. He made Italian Americans like my dad proud back in the day.

Being a young Yankee fan in the 1960s meant that you coveted baseball cards of Mickey Mantle, Yogi Berra, Roger Maris, and Whitey Ford, among others. There were several ways to procure a card of one of your favorite players: by buying a pack of cards complete with a stick of bubble gum, trading for a prized card, or winning a card by pitching for them. I had at least one of each of these Yankees, and I acquired them through pitching cards. Typically, pitching was a one-on-one activity and usually several matches were occurring at the same time. "Topsies" was the most common game, with each player standing behind an agreed-upon pitching line (roughly six-eight feet away from a school wall) and taking turns pitching with a quick wrist flick, with the goal of topping one of the pitched cards before the other did; that is, covering any of part of a card's surface area, winner take all. Cards exchanged hands rapidly in topsies, as they did in "farsies." In farsies each player threw one card, the card closes to the wall the winner. Farsies required a delicate calculation—throw too hard and the card might bounce off the wall and rebound back towards you, too soft and your card was sure to be forfeited. But one could get good at pitching it close to the wall, and occasionally, after much scrutiny, a tie might be declared. "Knocksies" offered a different challenge. Each player contributed an agreed upon number of cards to stand against the wall. Each player pitched to upend the standing cards and if you were successful knocking one down then you kept your turn. Knocksies was a little like bowling—occasionally you knocked down two cards at once and the last lonely card, like one pin left standing, was sometimes elusive, driving up the tension and forcing you to bend your knees a little more and squint before letting fly.

I amassed quite a collection of cards while at St. Mary's Elementary; but I wasn't thinking about their future value as collectibles. Pitching baseball cards immersed me in an activity that nurtured an intimate connection to the world of baseball and that was enough. Strangely, when we moved from Providence to North Providence, I discovered that pitching cards was not as universal as I supposed it must be—the kids there didn't play. So my cards stayed largely out of view in a Keds shoe box, which I still have, although I've given my daughter my 1956 Willie Mays card. It's not in great condition, having bounced off a brick wall an incalculable number of times; but it is an artifact of my card-pitching days as well as my captivation with players like the great "Say Hey Kid" who used to play stickball with kids in Harlem in New York City. I built and painted a model of the famous catch Willie made during the first game of the World Series at the New York Giants Polo Grounds in 1954, his back to the ball, arms outstretched, his athletic grace concentrated in a single pose. Amazing.

My loyalty to the Yankees shifted to the Red Sox decisively during the "impossible dream" season of 1967, when I was twelve years old and a full-fledged member of the baseball cognoscenti. My conversion was complete and irreversible. The Sox won the American League pennant that year behind the pitching of Jim Lonborg and the tremendous all-around play of Carl Yastrzemski. I will forever be able to recite from memory Yaz's stats from that year: a .326 batting average with forty-four home runs and 121 runs batted in. He led the league in these categories (tied with Harmon Killebrew in home runs), qualifying him for a rare "triple crown." He had ten hits in his last thirteen at-bats to propel the Sox to a one-game lead over their rivals and the pennant, and he was declared the most valuable player. The Red Sox didn't win the World Series, losing to the St. Louis Cardinals in seven games; but it was a phenomenal season for him and the team and gave the Sox a permanent place atop the hierarchy of my baseball affections.

FALLING IN LOVE WITH BASKETBALL

But if the Sox earned my baseball loyalty, it was hoop and the Boston Celtics that captured my heart. I owe this love affair to my cousin Johnny who lived upstairs. Johnny was about eight years older than me and destined to become a policeman in the city of Cranston.

One day, with help from his friend Eddie Tobin, who lived with his younger brother Bobby down the street, Johnny put a hoop on the garage that was tucked away in our asphalt backyard. The garage was made of cement blocks with painted wooden doors in the front and situated with the long side facing the house. The backboard was a makeshift affair, and the hoop sat right at the edge of the roof with wooden braces behind, giving it a height of about nine feet, nine inches. This height was a little short of regulation but suited my short stature perfectly.

The playing space was a modest rectangle, with the back of our house, the back side of the garage next door, and a chain-link style fence separating us from our backyard neighbor serving as boundaries. You could get off a roughly sixteen-foot shot in front of the basket, and about an eight- or ten-foot shot on the sides. The longest distance was at the point where the driveway entered the garage area at a slight incline; you could chuck it about twenty feet from there. But you would have to contend with our family clothesline, which extended from the pantry window, where the washer was located, diagonally across the yard to a truncated telephone pole. The ball's trajectory changed a lot if there were clothes on the line; you could really learn the art and efficacy of a high arc shooting from there. But if you were shy of five-foot tall, and the conditions on the ground were dusty or wet, then you ran a high risk of misjudging the trajectory needed and watching the ball smear a clean white bedsheet or pair of underwear or one of your younger siblings' cloth diapers, a misjudgment I made more than once, to the dismay of my hardworking mother.

The limitations of our new basketball court did not dampen my enthusiasm for using it. It opened a whole new world for me that I entered heart and soul. So often I would run the three-quarters-of-a-mile from school to home. My little backyard had been transformed, and I couldn't wait to get there.

I think it was the following Christmas that I got my first Voit basketball and started to learn more about the mechanics of handling it. It was an outdoor ball, and for me a year-round ball. It didn't matter whether it was winter or summer; devotion isn't seasonal, and so I helped shovel off the snow as needed. My love for playing meant that the surface of the ball smoothed over within a few months. But even as the basketball morphed into a large rubber cue ball, it worked for me, forcing me to be that much more conscientious in balancing and controlling it so that it didn't slip away.

Like all kids starting out, I would push the ball from my chest to reach the hoop. But slowly I learned how to position the ball in front of me and then just above my head, with my right hand directly behind it and my left as a guide just off to the side. Slowly my body became attuned to the gestalt of shooting, to the combination of force, arc, and ball spin likely to result in a clean shot, one that dropped through the eighteen-inch diameter of the rim to make the net swish, an immensely satisfying sound. The process was more sentient than cerebral, more a matter of feeling and duplicating the motions for various types of shots—a layup or backboard shot, a shot from the front of the rim with the backdrop of the backboard to help you with depth of field as compared to a soft shot from the side—until it was part of you. I learned how my fingers could control and direct the ball as my wrist flexed with the necessary follow-through. My fingertips were the final decision-makers in guiding the shot; they knew when everything was lined up, making any last-second adjustment. Each time I got it right was a moment of exquisite equipoise. So cool!

It would take me a while to appreciate the lessons and metaphorical power of basketball. How giving and receiving and helping were fundamental to the game—for example, when you worked a give-and-go, passing and cutting towards the basket for a return pass; or when you set a screen for someone, standing between them and their defender, to give them space for a clear shot. How much practice was required to develop skill and understanding. How love for what you do can drive the will to practice, to get better, and how wonderful it is to learn that you have that capability. How much loving something is its own reward.

Sometimes my cousin Johnny let me play with him and his buddies. Mainly these were two-on-two contests; the space would compress us into a scrum otherwise. My shot was blocked often enough; but I felt encouraged that I was included, even if only to even off the numbers for a game. We mostly played "winners"—the team that scores keeps the ball. Each hoop was worth one point in these half-court games and we usually played each game to eleven points. Sometimes we would play "Around the World" or "Twenty-One." In Around the World you progressed from one spot to another along the perimeter of the court, with two tries to make each shot. If you missed, you would have to start again; but you could forego your second shot to hold your spot for your next turn. Whoever completed the circuit first won. In our version of Twenty-One you took a foul shot (two points), followed by a layup (one point), continuing until you missed. The first person to earn twenty-one points won the game.

My brother Rob and I played on the St. Mary's team in the "CYO"—Catholic Youth Organization—basketball league. We were both quick, but Rob was a mere sprout to my tiny seedling, and we were among growing saplings, so our playing time varied. Playing a full-court game in a gym was different from our backyard game. For one thing, there were more rules and referees calling the fouls; for another there was a lot more space to move in. We also wore uniforms—we were part of a team! And on our team we had "Broom." Broom was Norman Harrison, a reedy guy with a mop of black hair, all arms and legs that could move around like a flailing "Gumby"—the green humanoid cartoon character made of clay. Broom gave our team a distinct advantage in the paint; an opposing player trying to score in the middle was like Don Quixote tilting at a windmill.

FADING TRADITIONS, CHERRIES, MOM, AND FOOD

On its front side holding up the hoop that garnered so much of my attention, our garage on its back side was host to a sprawling grapevine. It was not clear whether this grapevine was ours or simply using our garage as a prop after seeping through the chain-linked fence that encompassed Kenny Capuano's yard. We didn't harvest the grapes, which dutifully hung in bunches every year, although I remember trying them; and neither did Kenny's family. The grapevine was like a ghost from an older generation—presumably Italian—pining for its ancestral home.

But it had cousins in the fruit family nearby, vestiges of an earlier vision for the land carried from the "old country" that still thrived in Kenny's yard. Kenny's yard was different in this regard from others in the neighborhood. Preserving a bygone time, it extended from the sidewalk to the far edge of our garage, with fruit trees and a thick row of bushes behind the fence facing Waverly Street. A peach tree and a pear tree sat pertly beside each other. But dwarfing these, with thick branches splayed out in all directions like Broom's arms thwarting the opposition in basketball, was the cherry tree.

One year the cherry tree was so laden with fruit that we were invited by Kenny's family to help harvest the bounty. Rob and I disappeared into the branches, eager to participate, scurrying down like squirrels to fill Mom's paper grocery bags from the A&P supermarket. We hauled away three or four full bags and feasted back home for days.

The idea of picking fruit wasn't new to us. In true New England fashion, Mom and Dad had taken us fall apple-picking, the prelude to Mom's scrumptious apple pies. But cherry-picking in Kenny's backyard linked us more intimately, even if only for a moment, to a way of life oriented to orchard and garden.

A few other customs of the past lingered in our present, some fading echoes of a less industrialized and more commercially decentralized time. Among the most noteworthy was the periodic appearance of "the fishman" on our street, slowly circulating in a truck while calling out "Fish, fresh fish!" With fish from Narragansett Bay and the Atlantic readily available, fish sellers had apparently circulated in Providence for a long time, finding a ready market among its ethnic communities. We usually heard the call of the fishman on Fridays. Back then, the first Friday of every month was a traditional day of fasting from meat in the Catholic tradition; like many families we kept the habit of fasting on Fridays through most of the year. Meatless Fridays weren't at all a hardship in my view because they opened up other menu options. Mom would go out and ask for a piece of codfish or swordfish or some other available species, the fishman would weigh it on a hanging scale, and the main course for Friday's meal was secured.

Fare from the sea otherwise entered our lives on summer trips to Narragansett and Galilee. On day trips we would turn left off Route 108, anticipating the moment when we crested the short hill that would open us wide to a view of the Atlantic Ocean, glistening with countless sparkles of sunlight that made our eyes squint, on our way to Scarborough Beach. Mom packed meatball sandwiches for lunch or prepared to mass produce peanut butter and jelly sandwiches, something she did deftly on her lap, and which we would eat on the boardwalk, punctuated with a crunch now and then caused by fine grains of beach sand that inevitably mixed in. On occasion we would meander slowly down Ocean Road, past the grounds of Fort Nathanael Greene, for clam cakes from Aunt Carrie's, a stone's throw from the main sentinel in the region, the Point Judith lighthouse. Or we might go to the fishing village of Galilee, where the smell of the fishman's truck was amplified by four or five orders of magnitude. During the late-summer tuna tournament, a highly anticipated event in the 1960s, we would see giant tuna hanging by their tail fins waiting to be weighed. We lobbied heavily for a stop at Maine's Ice Cream in Wakefield on the way home—"We scream, you scream, we all scream for ice cream!" We did this more for the sake of form and tradition than out of necessity—Mom and Dad were as ready for a cone as we were.

Counterparts to the fishman included the milkman and the ragman. The delivery of milk in sterilized glass bottles became more widespread in the area around mid-century. We had a tin (I think it was tin) milk box sitting outside the back door where the bottles appeared regularly. The advent of the ragman apparently coincided with the need for cloth in places like textile mills for purposes such as cleaning. The ragman was an integral part of this recycling practice, calling out "rags! rags!" and handing over a few coins in exchange for whatever we gave. Of the fishman, the milkman, and the ragman, the milkman endured the longest, supplanted as the sixties waned and more cost-effective supermarkets proliferated along with cars to get to them.

If we lived more in the ebb than in the flow of some old customs, our gastronomic lives were a loud exception. Food was past and prologue, present and future. Through generations of our family, through the vicissitudes and vagaries, food kept a steady course. Faith, family, and education were central pillars of our lives, but all of them had an inextricable and inviolable relationship with food. Even as our faith lives flowed with the rhythm of religious holidays, our birthdays came and went, and graduations finally happened, food kept the beat, food was there to mark the occasion. Food was the metronome of our daily and seasonal lives.

There is no greater example in our family lore of the integral relationship of food tradition to our physical and spiritual well-being than the Thanksgiving story of the moribund apple pie. Mom's apple pie, at least as good as her mom's, was regarded with reverence. It also was coveted—no one was surprised when brother Joe, the only one of us to reach six feet in height (just barely) and play football like Dad, one day inhaled a whole one without apology, leaving behind nothing but a tantalizing whiff of cooked apple and cinnamon. Mom, for whom Joe was still the little guy who clung to her after his ejection from kindergarten, was more forgiving than Dad and the rest of us, making two pies the next time. Sister Kathy took up the culinary mantle after we lost Mom, and the tradition of apple pies for Thanksgiving continued uninterrupted. One Thanksgiving, as Kathy's apple pie was making a short transit from one table to another, it flew in the air. For a moment everything slowed down. Then the glass pie plate shattered on the hard kitchen floor. Compelled by a strong sense of urgency, in an instant brother Joe and I, soon joined by Dad, were on our hands and knees in a desperate attempt to separate minute shards of glass from clumps of mushy filling and crust, licking some off our fingers and salvaging every morsel we could.

Our weekly menus were predictable, reliable, life-sustaining, and overwhelmingly Italian. By the time we arrived home on a Tuesday, the aroma of Mom's fresh meat sauce, just thick enough with a combination of tomato paste, crushed tomatoes, and water, and brimming with handmade meatballs interspersed with several links of Italian sweet sausage, had suffused the air, greeting us like a warm embrace. We couldn't wait for the signal that dinner was ready, sometimes delivered with Dad's playful stentorian announcement, using an Italian version of our names—"Tommaso! Roberto! Kath-a-leen! Giuseppe!" There was no religious experience more ecstatic than Dad eating spaghetti with Mom's fresh sauce. I'm pretty sure this is an inheritable trait because it felt like a religious experience to me, too.

That sauce was calculated to sustain us for a week, with spaghetti kicking off three days of pasta—Tuesday, Thursday, and Sunday. But Mom's big pot of sauce barely met the challenge as our appetites increased through our teenage years, with two pounds of pasta at a sitting the norm, and sometimes on Sunday she had to add water to stretch what was left. Mondays and Wednesdays might vary slightly, but basically dinners were a meat (usually pot roast with gravy or pork chops), potatoes (usually mashed but sometimes baked or roasted), and vegetable (peas, broccoli, or carrots) affair, reflecting Mom's own Irish and to some extent her French-Canadian heritage. Mom had mastered the Italian cuisine of Dad's family to the point that it was indistinguishable, and even if it wasn't, it was the best for us. Fridays? Well, pasta fagioli—a simple and nutritious combination of tomato sauce flavored by sauteed onion, parsley, salt, and a touch of pepper and garbanzo or cannellini beans—was a favorite, alternating with a frittata of eggs, potatoes, and onions or fish and chips that we sometimes imported. Saturdays were pure Americana—hot dogs or hamburgers and canned baked beans. Making Mom's sauce and pasta fagioli was an essential life skill that all of us acquired; it remains the smell and taste of home and the abiding presence of Mom.

Mom was the steady stream that kept our daily lives flowing smoothly. She was the warm and bright smile that captured Dad's heart and adoration back in the day. Whereas I might squeeze next to Dad to draw off some of the heat Dad radiated, I would go to Mom for a dose of comfort and acceptance, especially if felled by a childhood fever. She was a half-hearted disciplinarian, threatening us with her thick wedding band or "the strap," with virtually no follow-through but good effect, in part because we were concerned by the prospect of Dad finding out about whatever red line we crossed. Dad gave us a very short leash when it came to Mom; annoying Mom was sure to fire up his paternal ire.

The kitchen was Mom's domain. At our Waverly Street home, the kitchen included a short pantry with shellacked cabinets and drawers, a short counter space, and a washing machine next to the window that opened to the clothesline and our backyard basketball court. The washing machine extended the counter space as needed; when Mom was ambitious it might host some homemade egg noodles on kitchen towels. Mom navigated mainly between the pantry and the stove, which was in the main kitchen area in line with the bathroom. In this small space she performed the feats of culinary prestidigitation that set the daily and seasonal rhythm of our lives. Thanksgiving was turkey and mashed potatoes and vegetables, but also an antipasto salad and Italian escarole-and-bean or escarole-and-mini-meatball soup. On Christmas we could count on Italian prune pie or prune cookies and egg biscuits after lasagna.

Easter was a multidimensional feast, mixing the secular and commercial with religious observance. It began with a hunt for small chocolate eggs hidden throughout the dining and living rooms, some hidden in plain sight on doorknobs or windowsills or dining room chairs, small eager hands scooping them up. Easter baskets with large chocolate bunnies were more visible. For a light breakfast we might break the Lenten fast by sampling Mom's Easter desserts, Dad supervising. Then, in what must have been as big a revel as any of the year for Mom, we dressed for Mass. We have a short film clip taken by Dad with the eight-millimeter camera Mom gave him, with Mom descending the steps in front of our Waverly Street house, smiling and bedecked in a suit topped by a flowered Easter hat, surrounded by her young boys uncomfortable in their Munchkin-like suits, and Kathy resplendent in a white dress. Easter dinner featured a traditional ham, but for some of us the ricotta and rice pies were the stars of the meal, the ricotta flecked with bits of orange rind and chocolate shaved from a Hershey's chocolate bar. Dad would try to extend the life of those pies for days by slowly slicing off what he called "slivers" and serving them up to our incredulous eyes; it drove us crazy.

St. Patrick's Day triggered Mom's Irish reflexes, resulting in a traditional Irish "boiled dinner" of corned beef, potatoes, cabbage, and carrots. Birthdays featured a large Italian sponge cake layered with yellow and chocolate cream and peaches. Kathy preferred Mom's chocolate cake instead, an exception that her brothers accepted grudgingly. The sponge cake had an impressive radius. Slices rotated around a sizable center portion, whose sovereignty was often a point of contention. For years the only deviation from this pattern was for graduations, when we would go to the Twin Oaks restaurant in Cranston for some veal parmesan.

Mom only relinquished the kitchen on Friday nights when Dad and a few of his buddies—mainly Bill Morro, Lou Folcarelli, Louie Gigoletti, and Herman Rose—would gather to play cards. One day Bill dropped some pennies on the floor and decided to let them stay for "the kids" to discover on Saturday morning. This became a weekly tradition and for Rob and me, before Kathy and Joe were old enough to appreciate the mysterious bounty on the floor, our first source of steady cash.

I wish I knew better the extent to which Mom ever imagined her life outside the domestic sphere. She had hoped to go to junior college from St. Mary's, but her family finances didn't allow it, and there was little family will or push in that direction; not unusual for their generation, especially for women, they simply had no direct experience or expectation regarding advanced education. Grandpa Degnan's family had Irish immigrant roots dating to the second half of the nineteenth century. Grandma Degnan's family arrived later via Spencer, Massachusetts and the province of Quebec, like many French-Canadian families drawn to New England by the prospect of mill work. They both started working at a young age, and Grandma was in her mid-teens when they married. A couple of Grandma's fingers were casualties of mill work, and she would wag their stubby remainders at you with her cackling laugh. Mom was a skilled typist and worked enough to supply herself with the fresh fashion she loved to wear; but she left work life behind soon after she married Dad in 1950, enduring, sadly, several miscarriages before my arrival.

Mom clearly had other interests, some more dormant than others in our household of four children with a penchant for sports. Unlike Dad, she preferred movies and novels to the newspaper and politics. She and my grandmother and Auntie Ginny loved playing cards together, often for nickels and dimes; occasionally I'd catch them at the kitchen table, my grandmother announcing, "My nickel!" and the three of them laughing uproariously at this gesture they knew so well, overcome by the sheer joy of playing.

When Mom dusted off an athletic skill, she gave us a momentary glimpse of her youth, of her as a person not just a presence for us. Mom's movement was more compact and contained than free and dynamic. She had played softball in high school, was a solid skater and swimmer, and always seemed to match the beat on the dance floor, whether dancing a two-step pattern, swing, or the cha-cha-cha, her ease conditioned by trips to the ballroom at Rhodes-on-the-Pawtuxet in Cranston with Dad before they were married (alas—only Kathy inherited our parents' aptitude for dance). I remember her now and then turning on the TV during the day to do exercises in concert with Jack LaLanne, a remarkable fitness guru, the first to host a TV show. For years she participated in a weekly duck-pin bowling league, her average above one hundred and well above Dad's, whose style was a wild gallop compared to Mom's steady gait.

MY RELATIONSHIP TO SWEARING AND OTHER MORAL CONCERNS

My Catholic upbringing led me, for a time, to see the world in simple binary terms—sin/virtue; mortal sin (intentional and severe)/venial sin (much less grievous but also nebulous, so it was hard to know when you were committing one); right/wrong; heaven/hell. This dichotomizing of behavior occasionally caused me inner turmoil, fueled by worry that I might transgress in the wrong direction. For sure, if you sink into this binary world too deeply, you can feel an intolerable pressure on the heart and soul. You can start to police yourself, an annoying habit that can imprison rather than free your spirit and joy of life.

Maybe some of us put swearing in the right/wrong category. I took that position, taking my cue from adult disapproval. At a later time I was not so sure, but was still priggish about it, considering it distasteful and artistically anemic. My wife Elena would counter this last point. Fluent in Russian, she claims that no language in her experience can match Russian in the art of creative imprecation, least of all English, which she finds impoverished and one-dimensional in this regard. Like me more a listener than a practitioner of the art, she found herself muttering choice Russian expressions when dismissed or dismayed in her first efforts to navigate American culture and by some of the personalities she first encountered. As for me, I got in the habit of not swearing to the point where my friends would avoid it in my presence or apologize at a slip of the tongue. I sometimes felt the loss of the entertainment value and release of tension in those instances. But I might also tell them about my own occasional mutterings or at least about my most notable indulgence.

As a boy, I took solace in the fact that one can salve one's conscience by going to confession and showing contrition. This seemed to me a great thing. After I made my first confession—I must have been about seven years old—I felt free to sin; let me hasten to add that my concept of sin was very rudimentary at the time. So one day I decided to swear effusively in front of my neighborhood friends, assuring them of my salvageable soul. This outburst didn't last long; I remember it because it was like an out-of-body experience. I forget their reactions but realized in the aftermath that I was perhaps missing the point of my Catholic teaching. I would have refrained from such an expression of my dark side in front of my parents, and that told me something.

What I had to work on was my moral reasoning, not just my moral behavior. Relying on confession seemed to suggest a weak character. Why not concentrate instead on cultivating the habit of moral behavior and limit confessions to the less grievous sins, like telling the priest about what my maternal grandmother laughingly referred to as a "white lie" or about getting angry at someone and wishing them ill? So, at some point this is what I tried to do.

Over time I came to accept that I could not fully control all my thoughts. Lots of things came unbidden into my head, and some of them interfered with my commitment to purity of mind and heart. Some of the saints apparently confronted this unwelcome intrusion of the subconscious, and they somehow handled it; but then, they were saints.

Basically, I struggled with a flat-earth, life-is-black-and-white moral philosophy. Increasingly, my monochrome vision was coming up against a more rugged and varied geography. Life was rounder and more whole, and much more colorful and beautiful, than flat and sterile. Life was filled with hills and valleys, deserts and waterways; it was verdant as well as rocky; it had a visible light spectrum with hues shading into each other and an invisible spectrum, too. I began to think of myself as part of this broader, rounder world. At one point I wrote it all out, starting with me and my identity as a member of my family living on Waverly Street in Providence and ending with my identity as a member of the human race, living on the earth, in the solar system, in the universe. I remember being quite impressed by this expansive new view of who I was.

This is not to say that I was ready to throw out a moral playbook and declare morality relative—some things are clearly right and others wrong. But I was beginning to see that we are not automatons designed to measure each action according to a strict code. For one thing, a code seemed woefully inadequate in addressing life's complexities; for another, there was the whole question of the role of conscience and love in guiding behavior. Was loving action perforce moral action? Could it ever be the reverse, in which morally sanctioned action was not loving action? How would you know when something was an act of love or something else, like self-interest? Focusing on behavior might make sense for someone at the primitive level of moral understanding that I was when I decided to display my knowledge of swearing in the street; but there was a lot more to think about.

A prime example of higher moral thinking was in the biblical New Testament story of Jesus' response to a group of Pharisees who presented him with an adulterous woman, wanting to test whether he would condemn her to stoning according to Mosaic Law. Jesus turns the tables, asking those among the Pharisees who have not sinned to cast the first stone. When the Pharisees one by one turn away, Jesus and the woman are alone. Jesus forgives the woman and urges her to sin no more. Here was a clear case of sin and moral culpability, yes, but also a response grounded in a principle of morality focused on the whole person and not simply personal behavior. In Jesus's moral vision, peremptory judgment gives way to mercy and forgiveness and the possibility of a redemptive life. One distinction that I had to learn to make was between a legalistic and a loving response such as this one. Closely related was the challenge of learning to identify with someone in empathy rather than from a position of difference: how might I respond from a sense of shared humanity? The seeds of this learning were planted in my discomfort over a display of swearing; but they would take a long while to germinate and sprout.

My thoughts ventured more and more beyond the binary notion of morality that directed some of my early learning, searching for something that made sense, something more like a center in a more rounded world. I slowly let go of the idea of attaining some ideal state, which had the uncomfortable side effect of making you think you were in a position to judge others. I had plenty of help along the way into young adulthood.

The evolution of my understanding of morality from a binary view to something more mature didn't occur in some kind of steady progression or evolutionary leap. Preparation for the sacrament of confirmation placed greater emphasis on the role of conscience in determining behavior; but conscience could be tricky, influenced by social messages and that resilient black-and-white mindset. I remember being confused sometimes by Catholic teaching on matters like premarital sex, abortion, and gay relationships. I certainly wasn't the only one conditioned or confused by one way of thinking or another. I was startled once in seventh grade when Sister St. Catherine responded with "What did you say?!" when I used the term "*Homo sapiens*" in class. It took me a good while to work out that she probably thought I said "homosexual." Why would this word evoke such a response?

3

Youth

"Education is not preparation for life; education is life itself."—John Dewey

"Learning *is* life, a supreme experience of living . . . "
—Abraham Joshua Heschel

HAIR, THE LA SALLE MAN, AND A WHOLE LOTTA LOVE

If you were able to transport yourself to the La Salle Academy cafeteria, circa 1970, you might be surprised to hear Led Zeppelin's "Whole Lotta Love" or Steppenwolf's "Born to be Wild" blasting away. It just doesn't jibe with the image of boys sporting crew cuts and shirts and ties and suit jackets handed down for generations; but these songs dominated the La Salle soundscape then, reverberating from the juke box and shaking tradition to its core. La Salle boys committed iconoclastic acts like loosening their ties in company with the beat. They flaunted the hair code, with locks trespassing shirt collars and covering ears. They grew their sideburns.

The thirst for freedom and self-expression carried forth from the 1960s could not be denied. The dam was released and hair flowed freely. My 1972 class yearbook is full of photos of guys like Joe Potenza and Cosmo Della Grotta and Gary Corsini and Mike Piccirilli with cascading locks—our graduating class of almost four hundred was hirsute. But then there are a few photos like mine, my hair parted on the left and barely touching my ears.

You might conclude that I was simply a traditionalist; and indeed, the male hair tradition in my family was staunchly on the side of neat and trim. As much as this tradition stemmed from a view that a clean and sharp look reflected a clean character, which Dad vigorously promoted and Mom accepted, it also owed something to the preferences of our barber during childhood. That barber also happened to be our paternal grandfather.

When he arrived in Providence from Italy via Ellis Island in the early 1900s, my dad's dad took stock of the skills he took away from life in Sessa Aurunca, a small village north of Naples, and landed on barbering as a way to earn a living. He was very good at his craft, with a steady scissors hand that clipped with barely a pause. He also learned enough English to read the newspaper and carry on the basic conversation essential to a barbershop. Conversation between him and my dad was a mixture of English and colloquial Italian. The temperature would climb rapidly if Dad and his "pa" touched on a subject like Mussolini, the disgraced leader of Italian fascism whom my grandfather somehow found reason to defend. I think his defense had something to do with ambivalence about leaving Italy—defending his homeland justified the ambivalence and perhaps made up for a deeply buried sense of loss. Indeed, the one sure way to get Grandpa into something resembling a state of reverie was to delve into his deepest sense of Italian identity. He would light up if you asked him how to say something in Italian or tell you about a favorite Puccini opera—when I asked him once he closed his eyes and started singing, the only time I remember him doing so.

Grandpa barbered in the heart of the city. At one point he owned his own shop on Smith Street; but that location dissolved when Route 95 split Providence in half. He ended his career by assisting another barber at a choice location in the old Providence train station. That's where Dad took us for haircuts at the end of a workday, every few weeks. Dad, Rob, and I, and later Joe, would troop down into the station to the level where the trains arrived, along the way passing the mark indicating where the water had risen during the 1938 hurricane—well above the height of a regulation basketball rim—and hissing radiator pipes superheating the nearby air, which I found an uncomfortable contrast on cold days. Most travelers leaving the trains would walk right past the barber shop, ensuring a steady clientele. Inside there were several swiveling barber chairs attached to a white tiled floor, each dangling a leather strop for sharpening razors and facing a mirrored wall and a counter and shelves with electric clippers, scissors, razors, after-shave lotions, and short brushes for cleaning cut hair off your neck and face. There were chairs with black seats and arm rests for customers, with the day's *Providence Journal* and one of several magazines within reach.

It was in Grandpa's barber shop that I encountered stirring photos of civil rights demonstrations and the Vietnam War in *Life* magazine. I looked for signs of the heroic in these photos, of something that measured up to my idealized vision of our founding and our values, of something that would help me make sense of it all. I saw people standing up for themselves, people standing up for others; people standing up for rights I had thought universal. I saw people sprayed with firehouses, people dying. The war was confusing. I wanted American soldiers to show their mettle, wanted them to do well; but instead, I saw grime and grit and foliage as impenetrable as the purpose and progress of the war. I found myself questioning the purported rationale of the war to prevent the spread of communism. The idea of the war as a stand-in for the ideological battle with the Soviet Union troubled me; more and more it seemed as if it pitted the Vietnamese people against each other. Our country's continued defense of the war also seemed disingenuous, as if by pursuing it we could prove its necessity, prove that it was the right thing to do; and/or prove we could win, regardless of the cost to us or others. Protestors of the war in the streets saw right through that. The stark cruelty of the war came through most of all in the image of the nine-year old Vietnamese girl running naked and screaming on a bald road after suffering third-degree burns in a napalm attack (Phan Thi Kim Phúc survived after years of treatment, eventually moved to Canada, and committed her life to raising awareness about the innocent victims of war).

By this time, I was finishing at La Salle and on my way to another Providence-based school, Brown University. It was during my first semester, in fall 1972, that I decided for one of my courses to write a paper on Daniel Ellsberg and the ethics and legalities involved in his public dissemination of the *Pentagon Papers*, the secret comprehensive study of U.S. decision-making related to Vietnam and the war. It was an arduous task for me, more ambitious than any writing I had done, and the result was a sprawling account. I felt I better understood Ellsberg's decision, the personal risk that he took in violating the law in hopes of encouraging Congress to end the war, the first amendment questions, and the government's botched attempt to punish him in federal court by using material obtained in a burglary. But the truth is that I had a hard time being dispassionate. I had begun to question the very idea of war, reacting viscerally when my Selective Service notice came in the mail when I turned eighteen the following spring. I started to think seriously about the idea of becoming a conscientious objector, not sure how deep my conviction; but the draft ended, and I was spared.

When I set aside my issue of *Life*, slid into the chair, felt Grandpa's warm breath, and heard the clip-clip of the scissors, I knew and accepted what lay ahead. Crew cuts were the norm throughout our childhood, as sure a thing as the rising and setting of the sun. Only when we became teenagers did we begin to push against the stubborn weight of routine, balking and stalling with excuses. If we arrived at the shop with longish hair, Grandpa would cast multiple aspersions in Italian, interjecting here and there an English counterpart such as "billy-hill" (hillbilly). Occasionally he would smile in his delivery, but we never doubted his disapproval. There followed considerable hemming and hawing about how much hair to cut and where. This arrangement was unsustainable and eventually my brothers went to a more malleable barber.

When Grandpa retired Dad assumed control of his tools. Dad fancied himself a genetically endowed naturally gifted practitioner, illustrating his self-appraisal by rapidly air-clipping with the scissors during those times we indulged him, and by eyeing our heads like a painter regarding a canvas, with long moments between actual cuts. You would think the results would be proportional to the flourishes and effort, but there was often disagreement on this point, and we would complain good-naturedly about Dad "butchering" our hair. Thus my relatively short hair in my senior photo in the La Salle yearbook. I've kept a handful of Grandpa's barbering tools in his old leather bag, somewhat out of nostalgia, but also as a symbol of our family history and its immigrant roots.

If the hair code changed at La Salle during my tenure, the commitment to educating boys did not. La Salle would not become co-ed until the fall of 1984, merging with two all-girls schools. Even in the era of Led Zeppelin and long hair you were expected to grow into La Salle men. That meant a commitment to excellence in character and scholarly and athletic pursuits. If you had any doubt about making this commitment your own, then the Christian brothers, fortified by dedicated lay teachers, would remind you, Brother Timothy Rapa most of all.

A Providence native, Brother Timothy was short, shorter than most of us, but his stature otherwise was huge. He was rumored to have a metal plate in his head from a wound inflicted during the war. True or not, he did serve in the army medical corps, landing at Normandy on D-Day and eventually entering Berlin with the Allies. His reputation was burnished by accounts of a measured use of physical persuasion on occasion. I have personal testimony to offer. Once in the cafeteria a boy standing behind me in front of the ice cream machine tried to wrest an ice cream sandwich from my grasp. Indignant, I tussled for it, until my head started ringing, having dinged the head of the boy. When I turned, Brother Timothy was walking quietly away; I felt some injustice but admired the efficiency and efficacy of his quick solution. Suffice it to say that when he walked down a corridor, his hands clasped behind his back, his head nodding greetings, it was like the Red Sea parting. As our principal, he had almost universal respect. And when he reminded you that you were a La Salle man and had to live up to it, you straightened up and became more attuned to your potential transgressions.

BROTHER JAMES, AGAPE, AND THE WRITTEN WORD

Besides Brother Timothy and his confreres, you were guided in your progress on the road to mature character and moral integrity by religious education classes at La Salle. Thankfully, these were different from the rigid and rote question-and-answer style "Baltimore Catechism" form of instruction I had received from the nuns at St. Mary's Elementary School, which had been in force from the 1880s, dissolving after the reforms of the Second Vatican Council. At St. Mary's my catechetical instruction guided me through the sacraments of First Holy Communion and then Confirmation, the one signifying the awakening of my moral conscience, ability to distinguish venial sin from mortal sin, and awareness that I was receiving the body of Christ in the form of the bread wafer we called the host; the other my openness to the Holy Spirit—which I understood broadly to be the guidance of God's love—and readiness for Christian witness. My instruction at La Salle asked me to engage in more complex moral reasoning and reflection.

Looking back, our religious education curriculum at La Salle seems to have been influenced by a confluence of cultural forces. On the one hand, it drew from the new openness and challenge in the Catholic Church emboldened by the Vatican II Council; on the other, there was the malaise and restlessness and countercultural movement of the 1960s and the accompanying breakdown of trust in old beliefs, traditions, and institutions. This milieu impacted all of us, teachers and students alike, including the teacher who gave us the hot countercultural book of the time to read, *The Greening of America* (I forget who did). For us students, it heightened the uncertainties of the adolescent journey and our need for solid ground to stand on. The curriculum, too, became exploratory. It was oriented much less to doctrine than to the spiritual and communal and social justice dimensions of the Catholic life of faith; much less to teaching behavior than to engaging thoughts and experience; much less concerned with certitudes than with responding authentically to our call to Christian witness as Catholics.

This dramatic shift from the scripted Baltimore Catechism left much in the hands of the teacher. In my first year we had a book addressing moral problems that served as a basis for discussion. In my third or fourth year some of us read *Man's Search for Meaning*, Viktor Frankl's account of his experience as a prisoner in Nazi Germany, which reinforced his belief in "logotherapy." Derived from "logos," the Greek word for "meaning," logotherapy emphasized the importance to mental and physical health—to one's humanity and personhood—of maintaining a sense of purpose and meaning, whether by completing a valuable task or caring for others, or some other way.

Of all my teachers at La Salle no one was a greater curriculum explorer than Brother James Deschene. Brother James had been a lay English and Latin teacher for some number of years before he donned the robe of a Christian bother. I had him for religion as well as English, and was equal parts challenged, intrigued, driven to reflect, and grateful. Motivated by his belief in our ability to handle whatever he provided for our consideration and to think for ourselves, and by his uncommonly sincere and intent listening to what we might have to say, I did my best to discern the meaning of all that he put before us. I noticed, too, the hints of irony that sometimes played at the corners of his smile, as if everything we were doing was important but not in the academic way that we might suppose; that what we were doing might have actual meaning for our lives and for what I believe he viewed as the real secret he wanted us to discover—the gift and joy of life.

He tried out different texts, for example *The Book* by Alan Watts. Frankly, I was mystified by this choice. Why read someone who draws on Eastern religious tradition as a source of meaning? What is "the taboo against knowing who you are"—the subtitle of the book? On the other hand, maybe my questions pointed to the method to Brother James's madness.

Watts took us outside our cultural mainstream to see from a different point of view, to think in a different language. He forced us to poke our heads out of the waters in which the culture of the time submerged us like rudderless fish. Laboring with Watts, you encountered the idea that there was an antidote to cultural alienation, to the culture of the individual ego, to feelings of disconnectedness; that the world was interconnected and we were all part of it.

It was from Brother James that I learned about the tripartite understanding of love in early Greek philosophy—eros, indicative of romantic, passionate, and sexual love; philia, denoting the bonds of friendship; and agape, unconditional and selfless love, mirroring the Christian notion of God's love, personified by Jesus. I found this such an enlightening and useful way to think about love.

In English as well as religion classes Brother James was fond of distributing dittos—those handouts passed down the desk rows accompanied by loud sniffs as guys tried to catch a whiff of the alcohol and whatever else was used to produce the blueish-inked copies. These were all single-spaced and it seems that he typed them out himself. One of my favorites comprised several pages of quotations from Emerson and Thoreau, distilled from essays such as "Self-Reliance" in the case of Emerson, and from "Essay on the Duty of Civil Disobedience" and *Walden* in the case of Thoreau. I found these invaluable kernels of insight and kept them for many years afterwards. One other handout ranked as high as these in my estimation—"The Grand Inquisitor."

Brother James gave us "The Grand Inquisitor" as a standalone story; but it comes from Dostoyevsky's *The Brothers Karamazov*. Dostoyevsky has Christ living and performing miracles in the city of Seville during the period of the Spanish Inquisition—that frightening time when the Catholic Church tried to extinguish what it viewed as heresy with fear and fire. Whereas the city's people regard the appearance of Christ in their midst as a revelation, the Grand Inquisitor views him as a dangerously misleading figure and denounces him. Dostoyevsky devotes much of the story to having the Grand Inquisitor explain to Christ why.

If you view the Grand Inquisitor as disturbingly iniquitous, you would be right. If you view him as either condescending, self-important, pedantic, chillingly cynical, or satanic, or all of these, you would also be right, according to my reckoning. He constructs an argument based on the idea that the path of Christ is too difficult for ordinary people to follow of their own free will. People are basically selfish: human nature compels us to live for "bread alone," for ourselves. To choose the path of Christ means giving up what is natural. It means a willingness to give oneself for others and for God. People, contends the Grand Inquisitor, are not equal to the task. Instead, he says, give them what they need: "Feed men, and then ask of them virtue." Christ therefore is a bearer of false hope.

The message beyond the words is clear: it is not only human nature that Christ threatens, but also the Catholic Church's policy of infantilizing and managing people according to what it deems best for them. Christ, in other words, is a threat to the power of the Church, and so to the Grand Inquisitor. The Church is the true guardian and savior of the Church's children, not Christ. Christ is a false god, or at the very least an inconvenient one.

Christ listens patiently to the Grand Inquisitor. At the end he blesses him with a kiss. It's a simple and vivid gesture, yet also a profound response to a torturous rationalization. In my essay on the story, I emphasized the power of the kiss compared to the temporal power of the Grand Inquisitor. The kiss was a response of love (agape) for a man suffering from a lack of faith in love and in humanity and so in God.

Perhaps moved by the power of the story, part of my experience in writing my essay involved the power of writing and the potential of my own mind. I remember pausing from the realization that I had written something down that I didn't know I could, from realizing how a glimmer of thought or a barely felt intuition can blossom into an understanding or an idea in the act of writing. It wasn't simply that I took up my pen and something magical happened—I felt adrift many a time with my pen in my hand. But I realized that if I were open and attentive and patient then an inkling might not only emerge but take on form and meaning. Many writers have testified to this power. As Flannery O'Connor remarked, "I write to discover what I know"; or as Anne Morrow Lindberg put it, "Writing is thinking." Many teachers today hope students will discover this power like I did. They encourage students to write down their thinking at different moments, no matter the subject matter they are engaged in; it's a practice sure to crystallize or extend their thinking at the same time.

My moment of literary awareness planted another seed of understanding concerning the act of writing and language, one which would germinate with time and the nurturance of people like Henry David Thoreau, Emily Dickinson, Annie Dillard, Thomas Merton, Gerard Manley Hopkins, and

Thich Nhat Hanh. To that point I had developed a sense of words and writing as a form of play (think nursery rhymes or "Jabberwocky"). I loved trying out a new word, even if confounded when my enthusiasm wasn't reciprocated; for sure, sometimes I mistook complicated language for sophisticated meaning; but at least I was verbally venturesome. I understood the basics of expository writing as a form of communication, with an idea of some of the characteristics that made it powerful, and I learned a lot about that at La Salle. I experienced, even if I didn't fully understand, the magic and power of words and literature.

What would emerge slowly was my awareness that the act of writing not only can be a process of discovering and crystallizing thought, but it can also be a form of meditation—on the meaning of a word and reality, on language and experience, on society, on life. Just as in music, silences are important intervals in the writing process, not only as space for understanding and language to emerge, but also to consider levels of meaning. Words denote and sometimes connote; even more, they reflect what we humans experience and try to understand about ourselves and the world.

How often I've caught myself rolling around a word or thought in my mind, as if wanting to taste its contours and nuances. We tend to think of language in terms of utility and emotion and enjoyment. But there is something sacred about it as well; it's one of our ways of reaching out to touch and name and live in what is real, what is true.

LEARNING CHARACTER AND UNLEARNING FALLACIOUS REASONING

Before Brother James, I had brothers and lay teachers who accepted us in our relatively unformed state and who did their best to unlock the potential of our minds. By "our" I mean the whole student body, but especially a group of us who shared most of the same classes throughout our four years. They included my long-haired friends mentioned above and several others, David Brillon and Bill Shawcross among them. We were important to each other even if we might not acknowledge it, because we each contributed to the character and the ethos of our learning. To illustrate, I'll introduce a few of them, starting with Mike Piccirilli.

Mike didn't exactly defy the La Salle code of conduct, except on one or two notable occasions of which I am aware, early in ninth grade when we were still confused about what was cool and what was immature. He simply decided at some point to be himself, come what may. One of his wayward acts was a collaborative effort that included Bob Poirier. Bob sat behind Mike in alphabetical order in Mr. Fortin's freshman world history class, but as a lark they would occasionally switch seats to keep their identities a puzzle during attendance-taking, something they could do with little chance of detection in a class of more than thirty. Bob's joie de vivre sometimes got away from him; but he generally was a smiling and sane guy who loved French and soccer.

The incident in question occurred in Mr. Fortin's class. Clearly in love with his subject, which he often expressed in voluminous notes on the blackboard, vigorously applied, Mr. Fortin probably overestimated the fervor of his students for the material. In truth he sometimes simply got lost in whatever was at hand, whether Greek mythology according to Edith Hamilton or the emergence of the Enlightenment era. This was an admirable trait in most circumstances, but could distract Mr. Fortin from seeing everything happening in class, including moments when a student sought to relieve the tedium of notetaking. One day Mr. Fortin put his books and his briefcase on the teacher's desk, which was on a raised platform in Room 104. In an instant they all crashed onto the floor, the desk having been shifted to the very edge of the platform. If Mike smiled, I didn't notice, and he might have been one of the guys who stepped up to clean up.

Mike exuded a sixties vibe. He loved to play the guitar and composed some of his own songs. I felt strongly that Mike could have said more in class than he did; he preferred to keep a low profile, no doubt with guitar tunes playing in his head. When he made a verbal offering, he often rocked back and forth in his chair, as if ordering his thoughts to a rhythm. Mike's demeanor changed on the basketball court. He reveled in parabolic shots, sometimes scraping the rafters from deep in the corner, in search of the perfect swish. And if we groaned, we would also smile, because his shot was uncannily accurate. The three-point shot didn't exist then; otherwise, Mike's career on the court might have taken off.

In a competition for the best wavy hair, in any era, Cosmo Della Grotta circa 1972 would have a great shot at winning. His black waves descended lushly on either side of his head, almost to his shoulders. Cos had a considered way of responding in class. He typically would pause and blink rapidly for a few seconds, seeming to look inward for the right words (I related to this mannerism, sometimes closing my eyes to keep my thoughts in view). Cos was thoughtful and sincere, although sometimes I think he enjoyed making you wonder, because he could keep a deadpan look for a long time. He and Joe Potenza were co-editors of the school newspaper, *Maroon and White*.

One day Cos surprised me by handing me a book that he thought I might like, apparently found in his family's or a neighbor's attic. I am looking at it now as I write. Its cloth cover is red and wrinkled, with the red edges mostly rubbed off, and portrays two Boy Scouts, one peering through binoculars and the other holding two semaphore flags, arms stretched to form a diagonal line. Cos had handed me a copy of the "Handbook for Boys," an edition published in 1917, only seven years after Scouting began in the United States. The semaphore flags made sense—World War I still raged, and semaphore communication was still in use, albeit on a limited basis. Scouts could earn Signaling merit badge then and later (I did) before it was discontinued in 1992. I was amazed. Thoughtful Cos had given me a treasure.

Cos and others knew that I was a Boy Scout. And that I was a Boy Scout could be attributed to nothing less than the kind hand of Providence. Scouting was recompense for the loss of my childhood home in Providence. When Rob heard from a friend that a troop was forming in our new neighborhood, we both signed up as charter members. It was late spring in my eighth-grade year and whenever I had a free moment in school, I would take out my new Scout Handbook and study it. Once at La Salle I was recognized in the morning announcements for a Scout award I had received. But there might have been a less chaste reason, as reflected in a couple of comments in my yearbook. Trying to make some kind of impression, I apparently shared with some friends the words of a bawdy song that some of the older guys at camp would sing when Scouts weren't around. What I hope was more memorable for classmates like Cos was my presentation on camping in French class—"faire du camping." As a counselor at Camp Yawgoog, I had learned the value of a "gimmick" to capture attention during demonstrations. I decided to apply this teaching tool in my presentation by showing how to light a fire with steel and a piece of quartz. I knelt on the wooden classroom floor beside some aluminum foil I had set down for protection and directed sparks to a clump of fine steel wool—a surprisingly good substitute for natural tinder—gently blowing the whole into a flame and holding it up dramatically before burying it in the foil. I don't remember speaking much French during this segment of the presentation or getting permission from Brother William beforehand; but, a gracious man, he didn't seem to mind.

David Brillon was a bespectacled and likeable guy whose suit jacket tended to hang loosely on his slight frame, as if resting on an undersized coat hanger. He was mostly unassuming, sometimes with his head bowed, likely because it was weighed down by a congeries of complicated thought that none of us knew about; he annually vied for the position of top student in our class. He had a creative side that leaned to the macabre, every October telling us with eyes gleaming about his intricate Halloween display at his home on Charles Street, which sounded like an audition for haunted house of the year. David didn't stutter, but his words might tumble out quickly when first sharing a thought, most likely because they were being pushed forward by the torrent accumulating in his brain. By comparison Larry Cahoone, befitting his future role as a professor of philosophy, chose his words carefully and deliberately (Larry had some height and, in addition to the broad realm of thought itself, his comfort zone was in the paint on the court). David would go to medical school, ultimately becoming a professor of clinical medicine at Cornell.

I arrived for my first day at La Salle a little after 7:00 a.m., climbing the steps ascending like wedding cake layers from the corner of Academy Avenue and Smith Street to a set of three entrances. Dad had dropped me off on his way to teaching in Warwick. The building facade seemed both noble and imposing, and I had no idea what to expect. At that early hour I found myself alone and in a big space. I wandered a bit, uncertain and wondering, and then another boy appeared, also gazing around. We introduced ourselves and that's how I met Bill Shawcross.

I was struck immediately by Bill's long sideburns and saw them as a sign of maturity. Indeed, Bill seemed more self-assured than I felt, and I instinctively thought that I would enhance my own stature by association, and negate any false impression given by my smooth hair-free face. We hung around, destined to share many classes and play intramurals together, and to play on the same three-man basketball team during intramural season at Brown. Math and practicality were in Bill's wheelhouse, and he ended up pursuing engineering followed by a career with General Electric.

Mike, Cosmo, David, Larry, Bill, and others were with me in Brother August Stephen's ninth-grade English class, where I had one of my first mind-opening experiences at La Salle. "Auggie," as we privately called him, seemed to have one overriding principle to guide his teaching—he simply expected you to engage in the intellectual work of the class seriously. There seemed no downside in sticking to this philosophical course, since Brother Stephen didn't seem like someone whose stance you could question. He made this clear mainly by a look of incredulity if you strayed too far from your intellectual self, sometimes while struggling to suppress a wry smile. He was by no means heavy-handed, but rather intent on strengthening our understanding of things fundamental to literary work, like rhetoric, irony, and the power of the short story.

From Brother Stephen and Aristotle we learned about persuasion and fallacies in argumentation. Persuasion is built on three basic elements in the Aristotelian scheme: ethos, pathos, and logos. Ethos refers to the audience's need to trust the speaker, to character and credibility; pathos to the emotional appeal of the argument; and logos to the logic, the reasoning of the argument and what backs it up. Fallacies are numerous. Claim that part of something represents the whole or the reverse—that the whole represents the part—then you're in foul territory. Try to fall back on tradition, on the argument that it's-true-because-it's-always-been-true, then you're off the field and back on the bench. Not happy with how the argument is going and decide to shift tactics to attack the person making the argument? Then you are committing the ad hominem fallacy. Want to simplify logos by proving your argument with the point you're trying to make? Aristotle says strike three, you're out.

Studying Aristotle on rhetoric made you realize that you were going through life half-awake and that the half-awake part was awash in fallacy. Try using Aristotle to analyze everyday commercials as we did, and you'll discover the art of persuasion at work, often with total disregard for fallacy. You're told something is great because something is great. You're asked to believe the irrelevant is relevant or that something is great because there is a sexy person right there.

Maybe worse, you discover how much you use fallacy instead of clear language and lucid reasoning in your everyday effort to exercise your free will. How often did my siblings and I use the ad hominem argument as emotion took over from reasoning—"You're an idiot!" How often were we victims of false moral equivalency, charged with outrageous crime because we stole the last piece of Crugnale's bread or mistakenly got in the shower when it wasn't our turn. At least in domestic cases you could shift from fallacious argument to food diplomacy and offer to share a package of Oreos or Fig Newtons, or something similar.

Brother Edmund, a grizzled but kind veteran, tried a different mode of persuasion in ninth-grade algebra class where, pardon the pun, the slope of learning could be steep and slippery. After explaining something on the chalkboard, he shifted to a loose carrot-and-stick methodology. His preventative for you sliding away from your resolve to learn took the form of an iron rod that he called his "persuader," which he would pick up from the chalk shelf at the base of the blackboard and brandish; but it was all show, as the twinkle in his eyes would suggest. If he saw you struggling with a problem during seatwork, he would sidle over, dig through his cassock into a pants pocket underneath, and pull out a candy, saying he thought you might need it. He didn't coach you, as sometimes I wished he had; he coaxed you. I was a little unsettled when he handed me a candy one day, but relieved when, finally, the mystery of x and y and how to solve for them in an equation cleared up.

The math part of my brain was functioning satisfactorily by the time I made it to Mr. McNamara's "Analysis" class. Mr. McNamara was new to La Salle when we had him. I believe his teaching methodology grew from his innate kindness. He had a knack for knowing when to let things ferment in silence and when to try an intervention in the form of an example or clarification. He would often pause, run his hand through his hair, and stand quizzically until he heard or saw something from us that he could work with. He sometimes would hand the chalk to one of us to show or explain a calculation, looking on intently, focused more on our thinking than the right answer, aiming to understand rather than simply evaluate. He showed a genuine and patient interest in what sense we were making of something or other, and in how to chart a path from opaque to transparent in our math learning. These qualities inspired trying, and one day I offered to go to the board to explain the quadratic equation—basically my understanding, having just emerged from a dense fog, of why it was what it was. It was but a blip on the radar of the class, but for me a big step in my evolution as a math learner.

Other teachers did their part to move minds and spirits at La Salle. Brother Able challenged us as sophomores to learn history through primary sources, forcing us to engage in historical thinking rather than to accumulate information. Mr. Cerra—whom my father had coached in wrestling and still brawny—taught biology in a muscular way, pushing and prodding us to learn. Affable and accessible, Brother James Quinn insisted through his manner that we could learn geometry.

In my experience the teachers who moved us the most were those, epitomized by Brother James Deschene, who accepted and believed in us and wanted us to believe in ourselves, who saw more in us than we might see, and who communicated their faith by expecting us to act on it and by giving us something challenging to try and the room to try it, while providing support through respectful and attentive listening or a kind and quiet insistence, according to their personalities. In this way, whether we sensed it or not, they taught us a lesson fundamental to our education, one not concerning intellect or knowledge per se but rather a way of being, a way of regarding, respecting, and engaging each other as human beings.

JOY, DRIVE, AND CRANKY

My life in the spaces between and outside the classrooms—in the corridors, the cramped basement that included the claustrophobic gym and athletic rooms, the rooms used for extracurricular activities, the fields outside—had important moments but was not as impactful as it might have been. For sure, my life outside of La Salle, immersed primarily in family, Scouting, summer working at camp, and, as always, books, engaged me passionately and wholly, nourishing my being and growth in different ways. But I felt gaps in the nonacademic areas of life at La Salle—one in the absence of girls, and another between passion and fulfillment in sports.

One day as I walked alone to St. Mary's Elementary School (it likely was early in seventh grade) I noticed a girl walking ahead of me, her books held in the crook of her left arm towards her chest. I realized it was Margaret Talacko, and I didn't remember seeing her walking to school before. A girl holding her books up and towards her rather than down by her side like I did was a familiar sight (school backpacks were not yet in vogue), and normally I would simply return to my thoughts. But something in the soft swaying of her hips caught my attention. I felt a primal curiosity, a gentle stirring. I couldn't name it and it unbalanced me, but only for a moment or two. Still, I remember it.

Margaret had attracted my attention before, but for a very different reason. She was part of the trio of girls in seventh grade whom I've mentioned—the others were Rosemary McBride and Susan Ricci—who giggled conspiratorially and mysteriously from time to time, but who otherwise seemed genuinely interested in class and invariably offered responses that were on point and caught my attention. I couldn't quite articulate it then, but I was taken by their relatively mature demeanor and intellectual engagement, by their minds and personalities.

As I entered adolescence at La Salle, I didn't have an opportunity to develop further the appreciation for girls like Margaret or Susan or Rosemary that flickered in my consciousness. Except in one case, there was little effort to normalize the presence of girls beyond dance "mixers," no opportunity to be side-by-side doing some of the same things with the same wonderings and questions. As I would learn (and relearn), the side-by-side principle was a good guide, not only for bridging the gap between insulation and relationship with girls, but social gaps more generally; for discovering the personhood of someone you might have viewed as "other" or mischaracterized because of one of many social prejudices or fears that had crept unaware into your perception of the world around you.

One day at La Salle we welcomed girls from sister schools St. Mary's Academy and St. Xavier's to participate with us in a series of short seminars on a variety of topics ranging from careers to contemporary issues. The intent of this academic mixer was admirable, the execution, well, flawed. Barely able to contain our curiosity and anticipation, we were chaperoned through the corridors and classrooms when the girls arrived. We were side-by-side part of the time, but without a planned or relaxed opportunity to interact, we were muted—I don't remember talking with a single girl. And so we retreated, none the wiser, to our familiar masculine enclave, conducive to our growth in so many ways, yet also privileged and unchallenged.

I didn't dwell on this insulation, but I naturally wondered and sometimes worried about what I was missing and not learning. I didn't have an older sibling to consult, I didn't go to mixers, and I couldn't figure out how guys managed to get dates to proms, either because too busy (legitimate), too shy (true), or too timid (also true) to ask. Joe Allen, a genuinely decent guy, introduced his sister to me at a party celebrating our graduation in Mike McBride's garage. This meeting in fact was pre-planned, or rather an adventurous acquiescence on my part; but the ambience didn't feel right, I felt self-conscious and tongue-tied, and we barely talked.

La Salle was one of the sports powerhouses in the state, so trying out for a team invariably put you up against stiff competition. My hopes frustrated, I relinquished my goal to make the basketball and football teams after my sophomore year (I had a pretty good arm, liked to throw the football, which I had learned to do under Dad's tutelage, and did not see the disadvantage in my size that the coaches undoubtedly did). Partly, I was burdened by a blind spot—I had been enamored with the most prominent sports for so long that I didn't see my potential in the less visible ones, where my size would be less a factor than my drive. Disappointed after being one of the last guys cut during basketball tryouts in my first year, I tried wrestling, mostly because of my familiarity with the sport thanks to Dad. I stayed through the season, but not being able to qualify for the lowest weight class, along with a coaching style that was coarser and more cutting than what I was used to, discouraged me. Two years behind me at La Salle, my brother Rob ventured onto the wrestling mats, with their distinctive smell of rubber and sweat, and stuck with it, all the way through college. La Salle had a strong cross country and track program but not yet a soccer program. In hindsight, I might have focused on track. Not too long after La Salle I became a dedicated runner, although more for fitness and enjoyment than competition.

It was as if there were several currents flowing through the river of my life. The primary one, the one that always seemed present even if I sometimes neglected it, carried me forward steadily, with a quiet but creative and joyful spirit that I shall name "Joy." Alongside, sometimes in harmony with Joy, sometimes not, strode Drive, urging me in whatever I was doing. The pesky undercurrent was Cranky, turbulent and annoying. Joy kept my smile and eagerness to engage at the ready; Drive pushed me; Cranky poked and prodded me into moody meditations on shortcomings and timidities. Cranky could put me into an annoying state of self-consciousness, but it wasn't always bad, motivating me sometimes to act. Together, the Joy-Drive-Cranky River might more aptly be called Adolescent Experience. But those hormonal years just heightened their presence. And they haven't gone away entirely—I've simply become used to them and, just as when maneuvering by canoe or kayak on a tempestuous river, better at finding refuge and recentering in the eddies of life that are there if you look for them.

On the question of sports, with Drive and Cranky prowling along, I couldn't shake the feeling that I had not given my all, that total effort and mental fortitude were lacking, not physical capability. I had passion, but did I have what it would take to fulfill it? Was I too self-conscious? Too afraid of failure and competition? Joy might nudge me gently to accept the hard truth—keep your passion but it's time to let go of your dream.

I channeled my interest in sports into intramural play and writing about them, becoming the sports editor of the *Maroon and White*. In addition to some straight reporting, I tried to spotlight the less glamorous and heralded sports, writing feature articles meant to capture the experience of cross-country runners and wrestlers; they were fervent, if a little overwrought. I played most of the intramural sports available, helping Homeroom 301 win in basketball and soccer.

But I also knew that there was a little more in me waiting to be discovered and tested before I could satisfy Drive and subdue Cranky, and I resolved to try sports at least one more time—in college.

MIND, HEART, AND SPIRIT

At the end of our year with him, Brother James gave us one other ditto handout, and this one was the most moving of all. It was a graduation letter folded in an envelope, one for each of us with our name on it. The blue ditto ink is still quite readable. He greets us with "*Peace*!" and follows with a passage taken from a letter written "by a monk" in 1513 (as I know now, the monk was Fra Giovanni, 80 years old at the time and writing to a friend on Christmas Eve). Here is an excerpt:

> I am your friend and my love for you goes deep. There is very little I can give you which you do not have. But there is much, very much, that while I cannot give, you can take from life. No heaven can come to us unless our hearts find rest in it today. Take heaven. No peace lies in the future which is not already hidden in this present little moment . . . Life is so full of meaning and purpose, so full of beauty beneath its covering, that you will find the earth merely cloaks your heaven. Have the courage then to claim it, that's all!

Brother James writes that these words of long ago reflect "almost all of what I want to say to you today." He adds:

> To find in our sad world a group of people with the goodness and the greatness you have is one of the greatest gifts life has given me . . . Be a man of peace. Be happy. Dream impossible dreams. Love life. Remember: 'The way to become human is to learn to recognize the lineaments of God in all the wonderful modulations of the face of man' [a quote from Joseph Campbell's book, *The Hero with a Thousand Faces*].

Deep-feeling and deeply reflective, Brother James saw us better than we saw ourselves. His letter was as close to a loving embrace as he could give us. In my yearbook, he thanked me for "my quiet human goodness," cautioned, "Don't let life spoil you," and reiterated what he wrote in his letter: "Be happy!"

It is perhaps no wonder that under the influence of Brother James I wrote a story in my creative writing class with Mr. Ramsey that featured a ship called "The Inner Man." I was after some kind of metaphorical journey to deep human understanding; but what I ended up with was a meandering and vague story with a character so intent on inner experience that he left his human personality behind. As one of several students who auditioned to be the class valedictorian, I addressed the same theme, trying to highlight the inner dimension of the La Salle journey. I wasn't selected, but a couple of my friends liked it.

While writing this account of Brother James I searched online and was saddened to find his obituary. Brother James went on from La Salle to join the Benedictine order and continue a life of scholarship and educational ministry. He was not yet thirty years old when he wrote his letter to us. To me he seemed older. This impression may have resulted simply from my perspective as a sixteen- and seventeen-year-old, perhaps reinforced by my assumptions about facial hair—Brother James had a modest Van Dyke beard, something I was far from being able to produce myself. But just as plausible was my sense of his abiding faith in us and his seeming grasp of greater truths. Brother James had a combination of depth and lightness that suggested wisdom, and he opened this realm for you to explore as you would. That was his charism as a teacher.

I don't know whether Brother James ever encountered the writing of another monk—Thomas Merton—but I hope he did. About eight years after La Salle, I was drawn irresistibly into Merton's world. Almost every word of his that I read reverberated in my mind and spirit. Merton would add breadth and depth and clarity to the thinking that Brother James and La Salle cultivated. He spoke directly to my current of Joy and to the vital eddies of reflection and recentering in my life.

I left La Salle with my mind a little more open and inquiring and discerning, my pen more confident in the process of expressing and developing my thought, my voice generally willing but sometimes tentative, my faith and spirit mostly untroubled, and with a more refined sense of what it means to be human or at least the importance of asking this question. I also knew there was more to understand and more understanding to learn to live. I left poised for more growth—in my ability to engage more complex questions and to clarify and articulate my thoughts regarding them, in understanding better our complex social and political worlds, in learning to stand more firmly, with informed conviction, on my own feet, both for myself and for others.

As I looked ahead from La Salle I also felt that I was being stretched like a rubber band. One end was anchored in the structured and ordered and secure world afforded by family, school, church, and Scouting; the other pulled me forward, but the direction and destination were murky. I had a sense of this distancing in relation to my siblings, who were firmly in the world I was supposed to be venturing from; my next steps seemed bigger than theirs. I was naturally closest to Rob, who was finishing his sophomore year at La Salle, who still shared a double bed with me, and who would join me at camp for the summer, while Kathy and Joe were still at Greystone Elementary. I would feel myself straddling my familiar world and the one drawing me outward over the next years, sometimes with contrary pulls that played out in questions about whether to let go and go forth or not.

My immediate attention after La Salle turned to Camp Yawgoog, where my inner current of Joy flowed freely. I was eager for my third summer on the staff, this time as coordinator of the campcraft and nature center at one of Yawgoog's three smaller camps, Camp Medicine Bow, where Rob would join me. And on the horizon, practically a beeline down Smith Street from my house in North Providence, about two miles past La Salle towards College Hill and the "East Side" of Providence, there was the new world that I would enter at Brown University.

CAMP YAWGOOG

As my seventieth birthday approached, Elena nudged me to do something to mark the momentous turning of the page in my personal calendar. "Nudge" might suggest a verbal suggestion, a gentle hand on your shoulder; but nudging can become relentless when applied diligently over time, and Elena started early. So my ambivalence—whether to live in denial or embrace reality—slowly dissolved. And so it was that I had some friends and family with me as I started my septuagenarian years, together with some pasta and chicken and eggplant parmesan. Oh, there also was a slide show and a multiple-choice quiz, purportedly intended to highlight some of my idiosyncrasies, put together by a few of my creative co-celebrants, instigated by Howie Brightman and abetted by Tommy Allen, Donnie

Carlson, Kent Harrop, and my family, especially Elena and my children, Juliana, Natasha, and Andrei.

Except for my immediate family, none of us would have been there if not for the shared experience of Camp Yawgoog. That shared experience occurred for a couple of us over fifty years prior and for all of us at least forty years before. Captivating us at the height of our formative years, Yawgoog bonded us for life.

Camp Yawgoog is well-known in Rhode Island and indeed in the entire northeast, in words that have echoed through decades of camp lore, as a "Scout Adventureland." Yawgoog counts Rhode Island luminaries such as Governor Bruce Sundlun and Senator John Chaffee among its alumni. The camp was launched in 1916, just a few years after Scouting arrived in the United States after its birth in Great Britain under the guidance of Lord Baden-Powell. Camp plaques and signs commemorate a few of the founders and core leaders—people like T. Dawson Brown, namesake for the rustic gateway; Donald North, after whom the flagpole area in front of the Bucklin building is named; and Captain George Bucklin, a Rhode Island Civil War veteran and camp benefactor, whose memory Scouts salute while walking through the archway of the stone-and-timber administration building named after him. It would grow to become the largest youth camp in the northeast by the time I arrived on the staff in 1970, drawing Scout troops from New England, New York, and New Jersey, with up to a thousand or so boys each week distributed among three camps within the whole—Camp Three Point, Camp Medicine Bow, and Camp Sandy Beach.

Yawgoog has been blessed by great continuity in leadership, from the directors to the head rangers. J. Harold Williams, outdoorsman, writer and director of Scout shows, and inspiration behind many camp traditions, held the helm for most of its first half century, assisted by H. Cushman "Gus" Anthony, whose sense of mischief was surpassed only by his commitment to a smooth logistical operation. Rangers "Inky" Armstong, Al Gunther, and Paul Forbes together spanned almost the entire first century of camp. I was never more than one degree of separation from these founders and leaders. I met J. Harold Williams in a starry-eyed moment as a Scout, and counted Gus, whose spirit never flagged and who was the initiating force behind the camp's alumni association, as a camp friend as well as an encyclopedia of camp history.

Gus told many stories. One took place in the earliest years of camp, when Gus was a "junior officer"—basically a counselor-in-training. One day he and his fellows had what they thought was a clever brainstorm during a rare idle moment. They took the camp cannon—seemingly innocent and small on its wheeled platform yet with a big boom, the same cannon that for years snapped us to salute while we were assembled on Tim O'Neil field—and set it up, just after taps, with a trip wire along the path to the latrine. Sure enough, a loud boom interrupts the wee hours, and Gus and his buddies can't wait until morning to see if the precipitating force was animal or human. Tip-toeing down the trail, they discover a pair of pajama bottoms, and they were, in Gus's words, "fully loaded." When everyone is awakened by the bugle to stand in front of their tents for the morning flag-raising, there is poor Dick Nagle, legs as bare as the day he was born. If this kind of mischief was out-of-bounds—and Gus never got around to saying what the consequences were for him and his wayward pals—it didn't stop Gus from relishing the tale.

Having a personal connection to some of the men who embodied the camp's history and spirit helped me to understand what we were all trying to live up to and shepherd forward. That meant a commitment to spirited and creative programming, living the Scout ideals, and learning teamwork, responsibility, outdoor skills, and the joy of play. Like most camps, Scouting or otherwise, it also meant upholding unique traditions conceived and embellished by a host of camp personalities. And it meant cherishing the camp's 1800 acres with Yawgoog Pond and its five islands the central feature, adjoined by Wincheck Pond, named after the reputed son of the legendary sachem, Yawgoog. The landscape is glacially hewed, with countless rocks and a scatter of ledges overlooked by towering white pines and hemlocks as well as black oaks, black birches, and a grove of white cedars. Mountain laurel and blueberry bushes line the network of trails leading hikers to places named to intrigue the imagination, such as "Smuggler's Cliffs," "Ghost Pond," "Hidden Lake," "Devil's Slide," and "Sunken Road."

HOW I GOT TO CAMP YAWGOOG AND CAMP YAWGOOG GOT TO ME

Master-disciple stories are a staple of many religious traditions. One version from the Jewish tradition involves learning the Torah, corresponding to the first five books of the Bible and a source of divine wisdom. In this version an eager learner approaches a rabbi proudly to display his knowledge of the Torah. When asked what he has learned, he begins to cite different passages. In response, the rabbi directs him to return to his study. This pattern repeats until finally the disciple returns to say that the Torah is inside him and he is now ready to live it.

As soon as I entered Yawgoog, it began to enter me; it was a love affair from the beginning. When I arrived at the T. Dawson Brown gateway, I was mesmerized by its rustic charm and mysterious totems. It was as if a dream that I didn't know I had was coming true. My boyish heart was smitten, my imagination was captured, and my spirit took flight.

It was spring of 1968. Our newly formed troop—Troop 6 North Providence—had about a dozen boys. That timing was too late to arrange a week at camp for the summer. But keen to develop the boy leadership for the fall camping season, Scoutmaster Bob Vota convinced the troop committee—a group of dads—to sponsor a few of us older boys (I was thirteen) to attend a program called "Junior Leader Training Corps." Known as "JLTC," the training program was housed in the oldest of Yawgoog's three individual camps—Camp Three Point.

I could not have had a better introduction to Camp and the personalities that make Yawgoog come alive. The JLTC program leadership included Joe DeCecco. Joe's casual demeanor belied a philosophical mind, a wry sense of humor, and a stage personality that included rousing versions of "Flea, Fly, Flo" as well as "Dese Bones Gonna Rise Again," one of several African American spirituals handed down as part of the camp repertoire of songs. Among other skills, Joe taught us the art of a good campfire program. Our Senior Patrol Leader was Mike Finch. Mike was a vigilant taskmaster, responsible for marching us to and from the dining hall to a "J-L-T-C" cadence and inspecting our appearance to ensure that the JLTC program set the highest possible example for everyone else. But if Mike had a fierce devotion to his role, he also had a subtle sense of mischief that came through in campfire skits. What I couldn't know at the time was that Mike would one day ask me to become his assistant camp director at Three Point, and I would return to Three Point for a decade after having spent five years on the staff at the middle camp—Medicine Bow.

One of my favorite sessions of the JLTC program was conducted by Stephen Hopkins, a nature lover and future environmental educator who introduced us to edible plants. Stephen was passionate about plants and wildlife, including a boa constrictor named Dave that he trusted to wrap itself gently around his youngest brother, John. Stephen opened the Yawgoog landscape like a book and made the woods come alive. Wintergreen,

"Indian cucumber," black birch tea, and bull brier were on the menu he dished up, among many other wonders.

The door to Yawgoog adventure opened for me at Three Point and I couldn't get enough. I quickly formed a resolution to become part of the staff, although I had no idea what that entailed. Little did I realize the wonderful journey that would flow from my resolve, how much I would learn and discover capabilities that I didn't know I had, how much opportunity I would have to participate in and perpetuate the great traditions and spirit of camp, how much the yearly cycle of my life for more than fifteen years would be determined by Yawgoog, and how I would get to form friendships with some of the best people that I would ever meet in my life, friendships that have kept the good spirit of camp alight in my life like the Olympic flame.

FRIENDSHIP, MENTORSHIP, RESPONSIBILITY, AND THE TRANSFORMATIVE POWER OF PLAY

Of all the friendships, my longest and closest has been with Mark "Hoppy" Hopkins, another younger brother to Stephen. Our relationship, however, had a false start. It was the summer of 1969, the last week of the camp season. Our troop had just finished its maiden voyage in Campsite Scott in Three Point. I begged my parents to let me stay for one more week for a special program in aquatics, also in Three Point. I dimly understood that this entailed financial commitment and wasn't sure of my chances; but they responded to my captured and beseeching heart and didn't hesitate.

When not occupied with canoeing and lifesaving merit badges, and with keeping warm in my bathing suit at the Three Point waterfront during the crisp mornings that can visit camp in late August, I would walk to the crafts center in pursuit of leatherwork merit badge. Just as Scouts still do today, I entered through the gateway in the façade constructed as a rustic stockade, greeted with a cacophony of pounding mallets and a buzz of activity. The leatherwork counselor, a young but precocious craftsman everyone knew as "Hoppy," presided over the merit badge process; really presided—he struck an imperial pose. He would perch on one of the large workbenches right on top of the metal box holding the tools and assess your worthiness for using a tool before opening it. When I submitted my "Turk's Head neckerchief slide" for his inspection (something I constructed with strands of red and green gimp), my last requirement for the badge, he held it up, looked at it grimly, and handed it back with a slight shrug. I had passed, but there was little cause for celebration.

Hop and I had a fresh beginning to our relationship two summers later, my second on the staff. He had become the crafts center director, and I gladly left my role in the trading post to work with him and several others. Whatever lingered of my first impression had long dissolved. Hop was friendly and authentic, with a spontaneous laugh and an upbeat spirit. And yes, he had a natural aptitude and fine eye for craftsmanship, creating, constructing, and sizing up things in the material world with artisanal attentiveness and satisfaction. He was my alter-ego in skills and a kindred spirit in the desire to explore connections linking history, native material culture, nature study, and so much else. We discovered that we lived only three miles apart, he and his four brothers and three sisters on the North Providence side of Rhode Island College, just off Fruit Hill Avenue. We took advantage of our proximity to extend our summer camp relationship throughout the year, starting our lifelong friendship.

As much as I was happy to work with Hop in the crafts center, I was thrilled the summer after I graduated from La Salle to assume responsibility for the campcraft and nature center. There I had much more to offer. The lashed bridge with pine slabs, their bark turned upward, was already there, fashioned in part by an international Scout from Japan, together with a pine slab gateway to the area constructed by Jim Lanzi, who never saw a pine slab and a nail that he couldn't join permanently together (we were all pretty sure that Jim slept with a hammer in his bed). We added a signal tower and a raised walkway surrounding a pen for turtles, including a large snapper named "Lincoln" after the troop from Lincoln, Rhode Island that found him, which we kept for a time before turning them loose, the snapper raising its large triangular head to the air and making a slow beeline to the pond.

Kent Harrop worked with me and brother Rob at the center, along with Dennis Arinello, the most willing grunt worker in our group, a guy who would readily take the role of bull to your matador until you tired out. Kent by comparison had a gentle demeanor, introducing you to the plant world with hushed tones, helping you to understand that you were in a cathedral. Easily connecting with others and more conscientious and capable than he would acknowledge, Rob was an able instructor, an aptitude that would serve him well as a waterfront director at camp, later when he followed in Dad's footsteps as a wrestling coach, and in his career as a teacher of health and physical education in North Providence.

Kent and I were tentmates that summer. In that era there were still plenty of old army tents made with a heavy dark green canvas. Sheltering wooden platforms, they were spread to each side with considerable effort by ropes wrapped around outer rails and tightened with taut-line hitches. Most of the time the tent flaps were rolled up to keep air flowing and drive out any dampness as well as the mosquitoes that tempted fate by buzzing in your ears. The tents were an occasional social space but served mainly as a place to store your gear and sleep. So my attention was in full alert mode when one day Kent, a natural listener, decided to share his secret.

It was a quiet moment during the day—it might have been the "siesta" period after lunch or the brief lull before dinner in the dining hall. Kent hesitated for a moment, held up by the feeling of uncertainty that comes from sharing something personal for the first time. Then he spoke with a quiet sureness, telling me about his strongly felt vocation to become a minister. Vocation basically means responding to "a call," and Kent had heard it and felt compelled to follow it. He added considerable weight to his confidence by showing me the Bible that he kept in his footlocker.

Kent's authenticity and sincerity were palpable; it was a pensive moment. He was fifteen years old, me a year older. He worked at camp a handful of years before going on to fulfill his vocation as a Baptist minister, which he did without compromising overmuch his enjoyment of beer and banter with Rob and several others, a practice honed during nights out at camp after they turned eighteen, and later with close friends at Rhode Island College. Since his retirement a few of us have been with him for a "contemplative paddle" in kayaks, a centering practice that combines Kent's love for nature nurtured at camp with his spiritual ministry.

There is something emblematic of Yawgoog as a powerful educational experience for the staff in Kent's vocational story. If he had never gone to Yawgoog, Kent still would have gone on to become a minister; but Yawgoog helped prepare him for the journey, and mainly by supporting him in discovering and becoming more fully who he was and could be.

At Yawgoog we learned more things about ourselves and what we could do than we knew or thought possible. Much of this self-discovery resulted from growing in skill and in maturity in carrying out responsibility. Most of us didn't imagine teaching Scouts outdoor and leadership skills or guiding and evaluating others when we were as young as sixteen. Still less did we suspect the extent of our capacity for zaniness and theatrics or, more seriously, program design and development. I was not alone in learning that I could lead a dining hall in singing, act out a caricature of a character type on stage, organize a campfire program, sketch a weeklong plot for antics in the dining hall and around camp, or develop an outdoor program. Most of us stood a little taller and surer after each of our summers on the camp staff.

Whether in the dining hall, at a campfire, or on the waterfront docks camp was an outdoor theater as well as an invigorating environment for learning. Examples are legion. Consider Harry Dickens, a defensive back for the University of Rhode Island football team, who descended like a superhero from one of the skylights that used to be in the roof of the Medicine Bow dining hall (we were holding tightly to a one-inch diameter manila rope channeled from under his armpits through a makeshift tripod on the roof). Or Mike Fallon, a tall redhead refreshingly disposed to think before speaking, who donned a green jumpsuit, tin foil cuffs, and a helmet formed from an upside-down stainless-steel salad bowl affixed with a metal coat hanger for communication purposes, deigning to visit from some little understood corner of the universe, silencing the full dining hall with his opening address: "Mere earthlings!" Or Rol Deblois, an outlaw rethinking his plan to capture camp and, filled with remorse, emerging from inside a cramped space in the small portable and creosoted stage that used to hold the stand-up microphone in the old Three Point dining hall to confess forlornly to the assembly, "I had a friend once." Or Howie Brightman, with a venturesome spirit that occasionally ventured too far, a subtle sense of humor, and most of all a big heart, stoically walking the plank into the pond while playing a character called "Twitch" (with corresponding head motions).

But if there was only one program that I could see repeated, I would have to give serious consideration to the one orchestrated by my brother Rob and Kent. Playing mob bosses competing for hegemony over camp, they would arrive separately for summits on the little stage in the Three Point dining hall, Rob in an old black suit with matching fedora, Kent his counterpart in white. Rob would be driven in his Volkswagen bug into the dining hall via a wooden ramp. Brother Joe, working at the waterfront under Rob's direction, would emerge first to scan the area, bedecked in dark sunglasses and a heavily padded black suitcoat. Confident that there was nothing untoward in the dining hall, Joe would open the front trunk to let out Johnny Hopkins, Hoppy's youngest brother. Johnny would then open another car door for Rob's grand entrance. The summit ensued with a lot of finger-pointing, mock vituperation, and exaggerated gesticulation. It didn't matter much what happened after that—we were too wrapped up in the parody to care. But of course camp was saved from both.

Spanning fifteen summers, starting after my sophomore year at La Salle in 1970 and continuing through college, high school teaching, and graduate school up through 1985, my life on the camp staff developed a yearly rhythm that flowed as naturally as the seasons. When the calendar turned to mid-June, we reunited with veterans, greeted new staff members, and commenced a week of training that included opening dining hall shutters, hoisting up tents, transporting bunks and cots, setting up kitchens and outdoor learning centers, preparing campsites for troops, and refining skills. Each week for eight weeks we reconnected happily with some of the same leaders and Scouts from the year before, introduced a story and characters that would add color, drama, and laughter to the week, and coordinated learning, singing, and ceremonial and theatrical traditions. When the last campers left, we reversed the whole set-up process in a couple of days, then turned our attention to celebrating our summer together. We concluded with a banquet, staff campfires, slide shows, and an unveiling of the year's staff board, created by staff with an artistic bent. Leaving camp meant saying goodbye to incandescent sunsets gracing the pond, mesmerizing us and compelling me to get my camera time and again; to tranquil and meditative moments by the water or the campfire; to a togetherness that felt so full you thought nothing back in our ordinary lives could replace it.

I would feel a sluggish dissonance when emerging from camp life to adapt to family and school—"reentry" was like coming home from the intimate world of the space station and getting reacquainted with gravity. But during my ten years as assistant camp director and camp director of Camp Three Point I could count on a quick revival. By late October policies and programs and physical improvements drew our scrutiny, and we began the exciting process of assembling the next summer's staff. Then there was the staff reunion coinciding with the Christmas holiday, including a few days of winter hikes and indoor campfires and board games at the "East" or "West" log cabin alongside the Bucklin building where we cooked our meals. Spring brought planning meetings with troop leaders and perhaps a workday to get a head start on the physical set-up for another season. Once school or teaching ended, my attention turned heart and soul to camp. I often worked on programs in the room that I shared with my brothers, my anticipation and ideas bouncing to the tunes of John Denver, Simon and Garfunkel, and occasionally James Taylor, Fleetwood Mac, or Cat Stevens (now Yusuf Islam).

OUR YOUTHFUL ENTHUSIASMS AND THEIR UNUSUAL REFLEXES

When camp was over for the summer Hop and I went buoyantly from one project and excursion to the next, centered on our interests in native culture and craft, nature, campcraft, American history, and running our Scout troop. Our enthusiasms led us variously. We developed unusual reflexes, stopping whenever we saw a historical marker or historical cemetery on our jaunts around Rhode Island, and for a year or two at almost every road-kill; Hop had special gloves in the trunk of his car for that eventuality. I did not attain his level of commitment to carcass inspection, but completely understood and supported the connection to his interest in hide tanning and native decorative art. His biggest acquisition was a porcupine, whose quills he used to illustrate native decoration at camp.

We took a more conventional route to acquiring animal parts when we decided to try our hand at using sinew to attach arrowheads chipped from a piece of quartz to the tips of makeshift shafts as well as to affix fletching just above the notch where a bowstring fitted. We found ourselves one day at Rhode Island Beef and Veal in Johnston, Rhode Island. We were in unfamiliar territory emotionally as well as physically, as we discovered when we witnessed the journey of the cows from their narrow pens to the slaughtering room, where the carcasses of the cows were hung upside down. Stimulated by the unusual attention, the guys carving the cows—dressed in white hats, long blood-stained white aprons, and rubber boots, and brandishing long knives that they stropped repeatedly—were eager to demonstrate their skills. They competed over who could provide us with the best strip of tendon. We collected what they offered and brought them to Hop's house, where we dried them on the wrought iron rails extending from the little used front door.

Hop's house had a long history of interconnection with the natural world, with assorted animals in pens in the backyard and some internal guests such as "Dave," the boa constrictor Hop's older brother Stephen transported in a gym bag; so the tendons didn't phase his parents, who were also used to a miscellany of crafts and woodworking projects happening at the same time. Besides, they had a deep appreciation for what Scouting and Yawgoog meant for our lives and the lives of Hop's four brothers, all of whom worked on the staff at one time or another, including John, the youngest, often in Hop's charge.

From Johnson Beef and Veal we went to a turkey farm, which supplied us with feathers to help with fletching and other native decoration. We eventually produced some sinew and fashioned some rudimentary arrows and tools. But I had to admit that my strong commitment to authenticity and sense of mission regarding projects like these sometimes wavered in the face of the actual process involved. Working with Hop kept me going; and what we learned usually had some application in our program activities at camp.

Hop was very comfortable learning with his hands and paid careful attention to the details, working at his craft with reverence, just as I did words in my head. He had access to his dad's and his grandfather's tools, venerable instruments such as hand planes and drawknives and hand drills that looked as if they could trace their lineage to his forebears, including distantly related Stephen Hopkins, the Rhode Island governor who signed the Declaration of Independence and whose ancestor in turn signed the Mayflower Compact. We appreciated each other's strengths, how they worked in tandem, and how much we learned in the process. We mastered the art of making fire by friction with a bow 'n' drill, using dried pieces of long-dead Elm wood, and I assisted Hop in designing and silk-screening neckerchiefs and t-shirts for our fellow staff members, with Hop's sisters and my sister Kathy exercising their sewing skill on our behalf. We learned to consult different sources to inform whatever we were working on—books on survival by outdoor experts such as Bradford Angier and Larry Dean Olson, on edible plants, on native crafts and campcraft, including by men who informed the early Scout movement, in particular Ernest Thompson Seton and Dan Beard.

Where I was Hop's assistant for hands-on projects, Hop was my guinea pig for edible plant concoctions. Hop played his role with blind trust, since I was identifying plants mainly from guidebooks, relying on my ability to match descriptions, sketches, and photos with their counterparts in the field. Our taste buds ventured into mysterious realms of bitter and bland. The skunk cabbage was the most unlikely source of sustenance and became less likely after we tasted the bitter spadix in early spring. Dried cattail roots ground into flour sounded more promising; but our attempt at cattail muffins fell spectacularly flat—you would have to smother them in maple syrup to get anyone to eat them. Thankfully, Hop's mother seemed to have an endless supply of homemade baked beans and johnnycakes to offset the ill-effects of our experimentation. We were rescued from an impoverished meal on another occasion after a long cold, rainy, and windswept sail aboard a sunfish boat on Highland Lake in Maine, where Hop's family had a small cottage. It was early September, with the camp season put to bed and the collegiate year yet to start. Hop and I spent a week experimenting with edible plants in between hikes and sails. White water lily roots were part of the menu for dinner, hardly appetizing for two bedraggled and sodden young men. When we opened the door to the cottage, however, wonder of wonders, there sat a freshly made chocolate cake, compliments of an infinitely wise neighbor.

Hop and I were taken by Roger Williams's study of Narragansett native culture and language, *A Key into the Language of America*, which was the source for many of the campsite names at Yawgoog. We visited the Rhode Island Historical Society located in Providence's East Side neighborhood, where we were given a private viewing of Roger Williams's "root"—a dry thin stick about the length of a short leg, with an angle on one side that could be taken for a foot. The root was purportedly found at Roger Williams's gravesite when it was moved and was believed to have followed the path of one of the great man's limbs.

Our studies took a more formal turn in college. I took a course taught by the historical archaeologist James Deetz, at the time assistant director of Plimoth Plantation (now Plimoth Patuxet), which Hop and I had visited together. One of Deetz's specialties involved the use of "seriation." As he explains in his primer *Invitation to Archaeology*, seriation is a relative dating method based on the waxing and waning of the popularity of a design or style or other manifestation of culture. In the course, we used seriation to study patterns and their timelines in early American gravestone design from the seventeenth through the early nineteenth centuries. The patterns revealed how the designs followed regional paths of prevailing ideas about death and the afterlife. For example, the "Death's Head" design—featuring a grinning skull with large eye sockets often accompanied with crossed bones or wings—was the preferred motif for the first half of the eighteenth century, waning quickly thereafter. The Death's Head seemed to signify a grim view of life, an echo of Shakespeare's phrase "shuffle off this mortal coil";

that is, relinquish our burdened lives in death. The later "Cherub" and "Urn and Willow" designs suggest a more sanguine view, perhaps inspired by the optimism of a new nation. My developing gravestone literacy added depth to the observations Hop and I made at historical cemeteries. As a project in my introductory anthropology course, I studied local native basketmaking and Hop and I reproduced the process in his backyard, starting with two ash logs to produce ash splints for the baskets. Hop, otherwise occupied with becoming a technology teacher, took an anthropology course that expanded our understandings.

If we were more than casual learners, however, we also were presumptuous. We took for granted that we could represent native culture at camp. The most egregious example was our participation in "Indian lore campfires," complete with storytelling and dances. In doing this we were stepping into a long tradition at camp, one which we hardly thought to question. Only later, abashed, did we realize how much these campfires were performative rather than authentic. A few of our younger friends participated in native powwows, helping to right our perspective, and our sensibilities about the appropriation or misappropriation of native culture eventually became more refined.

Hop and I were companions in many things, including bewilderment when it came to girls. We both found girls and how to approach them a mystery. We tried to keep it light, joking about our ineptitude. One time after my one date in college we went to campus in hopes of running into the young woman, an exercise in futility. We were pathetic and we knew it, but we were in solidarity, and we had plenty to sustain mind and spirit. At some point we realized that what looked like an unbridgeable chasm started with small but brave steps; meant trying to act despite a stifling self-consciousness; meant putting one authentic step ahead of the other; meant, for goodness' sake, getting to know a girl as a person. For some, these were guideposts on an open road; but for the longest time we couldn't even see a faint trail. Eventually, in our twenties, we cleared a small pathway, and it got bigger. Hop was the first to make a major leap, right into the welcome and discerning arms of Joan O'Brien, and they are still going strong.

BROWN, MY DUAL EXISTENCE, LOSS AND GAIN

My process leading to Brown looks anemic from my vantage point today. For me, and for the kids that I knew, college exploration was conducted mainly by word of mouth or family tradition. These were supplemented by some brochures and a session or two at the guidance office with Brother Dominic, who managed to be both purpose-driven and jovial. Most of us acted locally and thought locally; however much this was a parochial outlook, it also was a practical one.

Our family college tradition was born with Dad. Dad saw Boston College and a Jesuit education as one of the highest mountains you could climb to refine your mind and character. I was taken with the idea of following in his footsteps to add to the family legacy. So, even though it felt distant in Rhode Island terms, BC was a natural for my list. The College of the Holy Cross in Worcester, another Jesuit institution, was a good alternative, with Providence College, a Dominican school within walking distance of La Salle, whose basketball team we all followed during the Coach Joe Mullaney years in the 1960s, filling out my college application dance card.

Then Dad mentioned Brown. So, we took a drive down Smith Street to College Hill, about five miles away. Dad's idea of a tour was to drive slowly, and so we hugged the curb along Waterman Street, pausing briefly to take in the quad through the archway in Faunce House. We then turned left on Hope before reversing course on Angell Street, crossing over Thayer. Hardly a comprehensive tour, but Brown had a big reputation, and it was in Providence. I added Brown to my list. I remember handwriting and mailing my application, another quaint artifact of my era.

In the end, going to Brown was not a goal so much as the best choice available from an academic and financial standpoint. The other schools offered me admission, but with limited financial aid. Although I was initially disappointed about not attending Boston College (my sister Kathy would have a similar experience), the combination of a Brown scholarship and loan and living at home sealed the decision. Attending Brown also came with the bonus, or so I thought, of maintaining continuity in the activity of my life that I cherished, mainly Scouting.

So I went to Brown, keeping my geographic center in Providence, but also beginning a dual existence that would shape much of my journey as a young man. My intellectual life resided primarily at Brown, but for the most part my heart and social activity remained with my family, my troop, with Hoppy, and with camp. The challenging question was how to hold onto these two facets of my life fully at the same time, and what I gained or lost in the effort. They were complementary but not always in harmony, sometimes pulling away from each other and causing unavoidable tension.

Usually, this tension manifested in small ways—for example, in deciding whether to spend a weekend working on an academic paper or going on a campout with my troop and Hop. The most dramatic example occurred as I was finishing my last fall semester at Brown. Although encouraged by a couple of professors to consider advanced study, although I toyed with the possibility of law as a career (mainly because of some prodding from Dad) and visited the pre-law office at Brown, and although I applied for a Fulbright Scholarship (I might have been out of my depth there, but it was so intriguing!), teaching always seemed my natural course. Brown did not have an undergraduate program to prepare teachers and, in any case, especially in my last two years, I wanted to concentrate on courses in American Civilization (combining history and the humanities). Still, partly to explore, partly to get a head start, I decided to take two education-related courses in my senior year, one focused on the psychology of education, the other on philosophical matters.

The philosophy course was a small seminar on John Dewey taught by Reggie Archambault, a Dewey scholar. Reggie enjoyed teaching, which he ended up pursuing at Brown into his eighties, as I found out when I contacted him by email about fifty years after taking the course. In our small seminar he might offer an idea or two and then solicit our ideas. His posture was often one of intense listening. He had patient and disciplined habits of questioning and nudging rather than explaining, of seeking clarification rather than recitation. This approach seemed to stem from his great regard for Dewey. Like Dewey might, he endeavored to nurture our own inquiry, adhering to the principle that our understanding would accrue in proportion to our own effort to construct it in ways that made sense to us.

Reggie also happened to have been a Providence boy and would-be beau of my mom's, which she blushingly revealed to me one day. If Reggie harbored any lingering feelings of disappointment at losing Mom to Dad, he kept them well hidden. Perhaps because he saw some of Mom in me, he asked me to take notes for our seminar and provide copies for the group each week. I gladly accepted this role because of the benefit to my own learning, not to mention my typing skill, and because Reggie could offer me work-study wages.

While I was in Reggie's course I awaited the outcome of my application to the Brown Master of Arts in Teaching program, a one-year program, one of the models of its kind, that combined history and education courses on the way to qualifying for a Rhode Island teaching license. Before acceptances were mailed out Reggie took me aside to tell me the good news about my admission. I hesitated in responding and couldn't mask my mixed feelings. Reggie looked at me quizzically and I muttered that I would have to think about whether to enroll, because attending would mean giving up my summer at camp, where I was now an assistant camp director. It was a real dilemma for me. The camp pull was so strong that I felt much more the prospective loss of that experience than of the Brown program and where it might take me. I clearly was influenced more by what I knew than what I didn't, but what I knew had a strong hold on who I was. I felt whole at camp, and that was a gift to my being and growing that I wasn't ready to give up.

Having applied also to a similar program at Rhode Island College (RIC), I did have a back-up plan that allowed me to keep working at camp. RIC made my decision easier by offering a graduate assistantship in their History Department, asking little in return except for diligent work in the small graduate history seminars I would take. I took advantage of the tuition-free opportunity and assistantship stipend to buy my first car, a used green Datsun B210. I was grateful for my new mobility, grateful to relinquish years of relying on a neighbor, walking, taking buses, and hitchhiking to make my way back and forth down Smith Street to Brown.

As if protecting my best interests, Providence—the Providence that bestows care or simply delights in happy coincidence—seemed to intervene in another way to soften the landing of my decision to attend Rhode Island College. I had some discretion regarding where to do my student teaching, and my dad contacted the principal he knew at Toll Gate High—Mr. Shapiro—about the possibility of doing it there. Mr. Shapiro gave his approval, and I was assigned Ken Olson as my mentor. Ken was a remarkable teacher, taking a disciplined and intellectually rigorous approach to his craft. He was a paragon of planning and purpose, writing objectives and notes and preparing various documents for his classes. But he didn't live in abstraction, monitoring closely the response and work of his students. He also happened to be the primary summer instructor for prospective history teachers in the Brown program. He was reluctant to oversee the student teaching of someone outside the program he knew so intimately; so I was determined to give him no cause for regret.

Teaching seemed to resolve the tension between my intellectual work and camp. It was the perfect intersection of the two, combining my intellectual interests with my youth-centered experience and enjoyment of creative programming. I was not breaking any mold in taking this path. Apart from the one or two professional Scout leaders who served camp, the several leaders who persevered for any length of time after college were usually educators. But my path would eventually be complicated by a third force in my life, the inner one awakened by my reflections on my faith and spirituality that caused the needle in my vocational compass to waver.

Physicists seek the "Grand Unified Theory" or "GUT"—an inclusive model that accounts for the electromagnetic force and the weak and strong nuclear forces. From the GUT they hope, as Einstein theorized, to develop a "Theory of Everything"—adding gravity and the infinitesimal world of quantum mechanics to form a single model. My personal analogue to this yearning for a unified vision involved reconciling my intellectual interests, my spiritual compass heading, and my affinity for the community and outdoor life represented by camp. Teaching, as Dad did and eventually as Rob and Kathy would do, seemed an integrating activity, and for a time it was.

But vocation for me was a little bit like the concept of wave-particle duality in quantum physics, which holds that an entity such as an electron can act as both a particle and a wave. Vocation can be a particle, something you can pin down and locate; and it can be a wave, something that is fluid. Try locating and pinning down a wave-particle and you are stymied; your effort at precision is held up by what the physicist Werner Heisenberg referred to as the "uncertainty principle." But that might be okay when talking about vocation, because vocation is not a question of nailing down a single career. It can have much to do with who you are and how you are in the world as well as what you can do; with strengths that can be applied in more than one way and that you channel differently depending on the context, depending on the possibilities and responses you see.

HOOP DREAMS AND ROGER WILLIAMS (AGAIN)

While Brown was primarily an intellectual journey for me, I also saw it as a fresh opportunity to revisit one more time my unfulfilled interest in playing sports. There's a lot to be said for naivete in forming a personal quest and thankfully I had it; because otherwise I might have been discouraged from ever trying.

Yawgoog afforded little opportunity to practice basketball. There was a hoop attached to a big oak tree outside the Camp Medicine Bow dining hall that leaned against the three-sided enclosure where Scouts and staff picked up and returned cleaning solutions and brushes for the dining tables. The main thing was to avoid slamming into the trunk of the tree when driving to the hoop or guarding someone trying to do the same, and otherwise to avoid an errant pass in the direction of the walkway that sloped downwards alongside the camp amphitheater towards the waterfront. But with a little effort you could stay in good shape at Yawgoog, where several high school and college athletes usually served on the staff. There were plenty of running routes and of course the pond for rowing, canoeing, and swimming. Some athletes brought weights with them to camp, too.

My resolution to try out for the 1972-73 Brown freshman basketball team had been solidifying since La Salle. But I had little beyond resolve (and naivete) to support my effort. Apart from intramurals and pick-up ball, I had been on a team in the North Providence summer junior league before I started working at camp, getting into a few games on the outdoor court at Evans Field on Smith Street. I hadn't had any organized team experience beyond that since eighth grade. I also didn't have a preparation plan beyond practicing by myself and in two-on-two or three-on-three pick-up games on the court through the woods behind our house, in Greystone. Still, I felt nothing to lose and determined to give my best effort so that one way or the other I could put my quest to rest.

Venerable and creaky and with a distinctive cupola, sitting across from the Brown football stadium and outdoor track on Elmgrove Avenue, Marvel Gym had important associations for me. It was named after Frederick "Doc" Marvel, an outstanding athlete and Brown's inaugural athletic director, the same Marvel whose name was on an award given to the outstanding counselor-in-training of the summer at Yawgoog, a recognition of his contribution to Scouting. The gym's sentinel held another association. You couldn't enter Marvel Gym without being stirred and straightened up by the bronze statue of a large bear, Brown's mascot, installed in 1927. The statue gained surpassing significance in light of its base, especially for a Providence native like me. According to its inscription, it sat on "a piece of the slate rock on which Roger Williams landed when he came in 1636 to hold forth his lively experiment of independence with strength and courage," virtues held aloft for Brown students that I needed to muster.

Two basketball courts flanked a central court on the main floor of the gym. Overhead hung a wooden oval running track, with a barrier and iron rail more than waist-high, at least for people my size. I had never seen anything like it and felt drawn to it. I would discover a pull-up bar, or at least a bar that could be used for pull-ups, in this upper atmosphere of the gym. The locker rooms were in the overheated basement, the domain of a guy named Eddie who seemed always there and who was the go-to guy that every place with nooks and crannies and obscure routines needs. Everything from t-shirts to jock straps were hung neatly on a central bank of hangars. The nasal-clearing smell of atomic balm followed you everywhere.

Having just concluded an outstanding hoop career as a forward/center on the Brown team, the leading scorer in Brown hoop history by a wide margin (only two have surpassed him since), six-foot, seven-inch Arnie Berman greeted us. Arnie exuded the confidence that comes from court accomplishment, and a dubious optimism that both the confidence and accomplishment would transfer readily to coaching and to his players. At the same time, he clearly knew the value of hard work and rightfully expected that of us.

Early practices were a lot of running frontwards and backwards, the latter while holding towels behind our back to discipline our legs and hands for defense. The suicides—each a series of sprints from the baseline to each of the major points of demarcation on the court and back—were prompted when one of us missed a free throw as we rotated to the foul line and kept us panting. A couple of times Arnie tested us on a quarter mile loop on the outside track. I was as sore as I'd ever been but could feel my body adapting, an exhilarating feeling.

Practices usually ran from 3:30 to 5:00 or 5:30 p.m. After showering we would take the shuttle on a mile-long route back to the main campus, disembarking at Soldiers Memorial Gate on Thayer Street. I would trudge through campus and down Waterman Street toward the Providence bus station. If the bus wasn't visible, I would keep going, preferring movement to waiting. Often I would walk up the hill alongside the state house, with its prominent dome topped by the "independent man" statue meant to capture the spirit of Rhode Island, to Smith Street before the bus appeared, there sticking out my thumb to hitchhike. I would arrive home around 7:00 p.m., ravenous for whatever Mom had saved for me in a glass pie plate in the oven, often scavenging for whatever else I could find. I might try to get to my Scout troop's weekly meeting, and I had a weekly obligation to teach religious education to a small eighth-grade group that included my sister Kathy. Every night I would struggle to read before going to bed.

I'd like to think that Arnie kept me on the team out of respect for my hustle and determination, the virtues highlighted in the official Brown press release to my local paper late in the season; but he also needed to fill out the bench. He certainly wasn't taken by my height or length, or by my experience in full-court team play, or by my black-rimmed glasses (which probably affected my peripheral vision, but which put me way ahead of my time fashion-wise—think Stephen Nedoroscik, the 2024 Olympian bronze medalist in the pommel horse). My understanding of basketball was more instinct trained by the movement and experience of playing than by repetition of specific plays or participation in an offensive or defensive system. In fact, I found it hard at first to learn choreographed play. I felt tentative while most of the guys, especially Dave Raila and Craig Scott, seemed to be fluent and fluid. Dudley Simmons, primarily a low post guy, could be dominant when he unleashed himself. His counterpart Art Schoeller was a model of diligence. Jeff Eckber had the most tenuous feel for the relationship between shooting and the rim, but he was scrappy and willing to dish; if you imagine the team lined up like the wooden bars on a xylophone, then Jeff would be one or two bars above me on the short end. Craig Civic and Greg Rourke were stout role players, Craig with a mind that to this day unfurls like a scroll to remind us of highlights and lowlights in our time together and of people and events shaping our cultural milieu. I had to learn the game with these guys confident only in my desire to do so and knowing that I would have to stave off self-consciousness. Reticence and persistence tended to be my default in situations in which I felt at the beginning of a rocky uphill slope and so they shaped my posture most of the time.

Each day I brought to the gym my love for the game and my appreciation for the opportunity and for the satisfaction that came with each small improvement and step towards more uninhibited play and in my physical strength and stamina. Seventeen years old, I was discovering new capability in my body. At some point during the season, not playing as much as most of the others, I started running a good mile after practice on the overhead track two or three days a week, eventually adding pull-ups and push-ups (which I executed as Dad had taught us). Arnie, known for his strong work ethic in the gym, joined me occasionally, going at his own pace, my head bobbing just above the rail, his so much higher. Soon I could reach the rim effortlessly from a standing jump. I never missed practice. By the end of the season, coinciding with my eighteenth birthday, I would jog the final leg of my day through campus and up the hill by the state house, my legs having grown so strong and resilient.

Despite having some good individual players, we never got to that point in team chemistry and cohesiveness where the whole is greater than the sum of the parts; we lost a lot. But the experience was expanding in so many ways, at least for me. We didn't travel with the varsity; but we had games at Dartmouth and Harvard, places I had only heard about, as well as at Boston College. We stayed at the Sonesta Hotel in Cambridge on the trip to Boston, and I tried walking to Harvard to explore it; but it was farther than I thought down Massachusetts Avenue and I had to turn around with barely a glimpse. Coincidentally, the Detroit Pistons were playing the Celtics and staying at the Sonesta, too. When we were in the dining room, Bob Lanier, whom I remembered well from his exploits at St. Bonaventure, entered—at least his shoes did. Bob was a walking tall tale; he was six feet, ten inches in height with size twenty-two shoes that could be used to ferry small people in a pinch, and his full form arrived about ten seconds after his toe came into view.

Providence College (PC) dominated the Rhode Island hoop scene. They were the one team that we could watch regularly on TV, part of the legacy of the Joe Mullaney years in the 1960s, with future National Basketball Association (NBA) players Lenny Wilkens, Mike Riordan, and Jimmy Walker, who led the nation in scoring in 1966-67. In 1972-73 PC had one of the best teams in its history, led by Ernie DiGregorio and Marvin Barnes, with Kevin Stacom as a sidekick (all would play in the NBA). Ernie was a legend in Rhode Island before he got to PC. He grew up in North Providence and was renowned for practicing by himself at all hours at Stephen Olney Park; in fact, if any fault lines are discovered below the park they should be attributed to Ernie's relentless pounding on the surface. Ernie wore out opponents with his nifty dribbling, passing, and ability to create space for his shot. He led his PC team in scoring and assists as they marched right into the Final Four, stymied from going further by an injury to Marvin Barnes.

So it was a real thrill to play PC at the new Providence Civic Center (now the Amica Mutual Pavilion). I had a cameo in the preliminary game against the PC sub varsity and then a front seat for the main event. Our Brown guys were led by a couple of sophomores—center Phil Brown, an explosive leaper, and guard Eddie Morris, quick and tenacious (the magnitude of both these attributes astonished me one day when we practiced with them). They surprised the PC team with their fire and heart, and had them up at halftime, only to bow in the end to their strength and experience.

I did get into some games and put in a few hoops, a few times with my faithful buddy Hop in attendance, and a couple when family members came to show support. Mom and Dad attended a game together at the Civic Center. Having mom there was a treat; she was nervous watching us at sporting events (especially when they involved my brothers wrestling), afraid that we would injure ourselves. She remarked afterwards that my legs were not the ones I was born with—understandable, considering I was premature by more than six weeks and, according to my grandmother, looked like "a monkey on a string."

While I might have performed better, I felt that I had come a long way in fulfilling my desire to play, and I was grateful for my experience on the team. And while I felt I had more athletic capacity to explore, especially given my high level of conditioning, I knew in my heart that it wouldn't be in basketball, at least not at Brown. And to pursue something new like track, the next logical thing, I knew I would have to devote myself fully, difficult to do with my different commitments represented by home and school. So I dedicated myself to staying fit and playing sports when I could, earning intramural points for Plantation House, the men's commuter house, in cross-country and wrestling (to win my 145-pound weight class, I simply outlasted an experienced but less fit guy who could barely catch his breath).

4

Young adulthood

"Our real journey in life is interior: it is a matter of growth, deepening, and of an ever greater surrender to the creative action of love and grace in our hearts. . . . we are already one. But we imagine we are not . . . What we have to be is what we are."

—Thomas Merton

A LIBRARY NOMAD, THE BOOKSTORE, AND GORDON WOOD

During my first year at Brown and beyond, when I wasn't at Marvel Gym or in class, I usually was in one of the libraries. The Rockefeller was my main base, in part because many of the reserve readings for my history and social sciences courses were there. But I was nomadic, changing my study milieu when it suited me, and positioning myself for different distractions if I needed them. I would sometimes go to the John Carter Brown library to sit at one of the tables with the green banker's lamps or settle into a comfy armchair in Pembroke Library. The John Hay Library, with its rare collections and manuscripts, occasionally drew me in, too. I tried the "sky-high-bi-phy-sci-li" (the sciences library) but didn't find it as conducive to study.

Low-lit, with rich dark wood framing the interior, the John Carter Brown Library was known for its collection of early Americana, and I knew I could take a break there to explore different displays in the glass cases. It had a very different vibe from the aptly monikered "Rock," its classical façade housing a scholar's quiet nook compared to the Rock's sterile and brutalist concrete counterpart. At the John Hay I always felt one degree of separation closer to Lincoln, since John Hay, a Brown grad, was one of his personal secretaries at the White House. I was delighted one time to discover there the pamphlet-sized scripts of two of the plays written and produced by Yawgoog's J. Harold Williams for shows at national Scout jamborees. Occasionally I would peruse the stacks at the Rock or Pembroke just to see what would catch my eye. But I was just as excited to take a walk down Thayer Street to the Brown bookstore to check the books assigned to courses that I would take or had an interest in taking. Taken together, for me the libraries and bookstore were an embarrassment of riches.

When I learned that there was a whole course dedicated to the American Revolution, my youthful vision of history as the study of inspiring ideas and ennobling actions rose up to embrace it. No matter that it was an advanced course; I was all in. Gordon S. Wood, author of *Creation of the American Republic, 1776-1787*, was the professor. I was enthralled from the beginning; soon I was overwhelmed.

If you knew Wood's book, then you had a major clue to the approach he would take in the course. His *Creation of the American Republic* was so evocative of the revolutionary period because of its impressive grounding in the literature of the time—pamphlets, broadsides, tracts, and sermons—as well as more well-known letters and founding documents. Wood immersed himself in the thought as well as action of the period to understand it; he wasn't out to glorify or sanctify but to capture, characterize, and contextualize. The course routed you through a similar process. Even as I worked to complete the required reading, I would go to the Rock thinking I might peruse one or two of the recommended ones, mostly primary sources. But the recommended readings were so voluminous, it was difficult to know where to start.

Gordon Wood's course was a vivid lesson in the art of the historian. There was so much more to historical work than gleaning evidence to match my own romanticized version of what should have happened; so much more than gathering the right blocks of information to build a rigid and unyielding edifice of knowledge. History was dynamic. We might gain better understanding of the past, but never fully recover it; and understanding the past was inextricably bound up with the present. Doing and learning history meant putting together a credible account of the past with the best resources available in the current moment, including prior work on the same questions or topics. Even as history involved consulting and weighing the value of a full range of sources, however, it also meant considering what was not there, what voices were missing, what gaps remained, and how the present might be influencing how you saw things. You had to complicate history before you could begin to understand it and represent it. Only in that way would you have something real and meaningful to say to help you know better your moment in history, the context of your time, and the future you wanted to help usher into being.

All my Gordon Wood history lessons were reinforced in classes with other great history professors at Brown at the time. There was John L. Thomas, who taught the American history survey course that I took. William G. McLoughlin led the seminar section to which I was assigned in his courses on American social and intellectual history; he seemed the embodiment of vigilant thinking and writing and I was anxious about meeting his expectations. James T. Patterson was a vigorous and captivating lecturer focused on the twentieth century, causing me to wonder how the personal lives of people like my parents and grandparents were affected by the social, political, and economic forces that resulted in the Great Depression, the New Deal, and World War II. The Great Depression left a huge imprint on my dad especially, leading to lifelong habits of frugality that he interrupted only when it concerned us or for special reasons such as his twenty-fifth wedding anniversary trip to Italy, which concerned Mom. Thank goodness for the "G.I. Bill" that enabled my dad to finish his education at Boston College. I wrote down as much as I could. I kept my notebooks from these courses for a long time.

MATH AND THE MISCALCULATIONS OF STUBBORNNESS AND PRIDE

I'm not sure when I crossed the threshold between youth and young adulthood. I certainly can say I straddled it for a while, more mature in some respects than others. The more mature part of me reflected my ability to think for myself, take responsibility, and stand to some degree on my own.

The less mature part was reflected in judgments born of some combination of overconfidence, stubborn pride, or blind faith.

Brown offered rich curricular paths but did not tell you which to take or how they might be combined. You did this on your own. This self-direction had its advantages, not least forcing you to have a good think now and then about what was important to your learning. It could be a burden if you were interested in a lot of things, and sometimes it felt that way to me. Looking back, although I might wish for greater exposure to the sciences, I mostly like the decisions I made, which leaned strongly to the humanities. My biggest misstep involved math, although I was saved from too much misgiving.

During my first semester I took "Calculus with Application to the Social Sciences." It sounded like one of those courses that would round out my learning by bridging two seemingly distinct worlds. I got an idea of what bridging could look like, but there was no obvious follow-up, and I didn't at the time see how I might benefit further if there was. Three semesters later I decided to take a pure math course, this time motivated by the idea that I might somehow qualify to teach math as well as history and English.

Ideation is a great thing, but so also is good judgment; then again, there's no living without trying. In this case, though, I was delusional. I picked an advanced honors course that fit into my schedule and fell behind the moment I opened the textbook, never to recover. I was befogged and abashed. I briefly consulted my La Salle friend Bill Shawcross for guidance; but it quickly became clear that Bill's understanding presumed a whole lot of foundational understanding that I did not have. Thankfully, Brown policy allowed for such failures in judgment, and the course didn't appear on my transcript.

Failure can be accompanied by many things—a sense of loss, mortification, self-admonishment, and even anger; but when you empathize with yourself and accept it, it can also be enormously edifying. I was relieved but also dogged by an awareness of how pride and my stubbornness, which in the best case becomes rewarding persistence, could obscure clear thinking and good judgement. As I had been reminded when reading Benjamin Franklin's celebrated autobiography in my course on American Literature, pride was a subtle and deceptive force. Franklin knew because he had tried to subdue it in himself, and it was a struggle; it threatened to upend his carefully laid out personal program for attaining true moral character.

Franklin describes his youthful difficulty living according to right rather than wrong: "While my care was employ'd in guarding against one fault, I was often surprised by another . . . inclination was sometimes too strong for reason." Facing up to his shortcoming, he resolved to attain to "moral perfection." A man of the Enlightenment par excellence, and a prototype for the American notion of virtuous effort and hard work as keys to self-improvement and self-fulfillment, Franklin formed a methodical plan. He compiled a list of "necessary or desirable" virtues to live by. His list reads like a precursor to the "Scout Law" that I had recited countless times; virtues overlapping with the Scout Law directly or indirectly include frugality, cleanliness, and sincerity. Franklin added temperance, silence, order, resolution, industry, justice, moderation, tranquility, and chastity, defining what he meant by each. He determined to give "strict attention" to each virtue in turn, with a clear sense of priority and cumulative effect—work on one virtue would pave the way for work on the next. He kept daily note of his progress by marking instances of faulty behavior in "a little book"; the number of instances declined over time. Thankfully, the Boy Scouts did not require such close monitoring of our behavior, although we needed to show our effort to live by the points of the Scout Law to advance in Scout rank and in leadership. Franklin's meticulous self-monitoring was his recipe for developing character and ensuring "felicity" in life, an ethic not only for himself, but also for the new republic.

Franklin added a thirteenth virtue, humility, to his original list when convinced by a Quaker friend that he was sometimes guilty of overbearing prideful behavior; perhaps he was too zealous in marking his progress towards perfection. Humility appeared last on the list, a testament to the challenge it entailed—he would need to call upon many of the other virtues in attaining it.

Assessing his success, Franklin judged that he became better at giving the appearance of humility than at being humble. For Franklin, the aspiration to be humble ran up against the persistence of pride, with pride all too often wheedling and elbowing its way ahead. As he remarked in his autobiography, with a fair dose of humility, it would seem:

> In reality, there is, perhaps, no one of our natural passions so hard to subdue as pride. Disguise it, struggle with it, beat it down, stifle it, mortify it as much as one pleases, it is still alive, and will every now and then peep out and show itself. . . .

If it did not lead to genuine humility, Franklin's determined effort was not without positive result. He tells us that he disciplined himself to withhold judgment of the opinions and ideas of others and to advance his own views modestly. He notes that his approach gradually became habitual and as a practical consequence his conversations became more congenial.

In realizing the necessity of humility for moral perfection, not to mention for tolerable conversation, it seemed to me that Franklin also discovered the necessity of accepting one's imperfection. He seems to have understood that moral perfection was a misleading if not false ideal. Striving to achieve it also threatened to put you on your own island socially, a lonely prospect. There was a twofold lesson here for me to try to absorb: accept more fully my imperfection and learn to distinguish when persistence was called for and when stubborn pride was not.

KNOWLEDGE, SENSIBILITIES, AND SOCIAL CONSCIOUSNESS

My decision to major in American Civilization (Am Civ) was easy. Am Civ took a whole-cloth approach to understanding who we were and where we had been. It was full of the spirit of the humanities, combining history, geography, literature, anthropology, and culture. It cultivated inquisitive habits of mind and an ecological way of thinking—the different subject fields were distinct but also connected and mutually informing in ways that I found fascinating to discover and explore. And it worked not only on my mind but also my human sensibilities—what it meant to experience and think and act not only from my viewpoint but from that of others. It also expanded my social consciousness, giving more context, substance, and range to the broad notions of morality cultivated in my Catholic education at home and at La Salle. During my senior-year seminar, I played around with the idea of analyzing what made the Boy Scout movement distinctively American for an honors thesis until I realized that such a study would draw away too much of my attention from other courses that I wanted to take to conclude my last year.

The formation of my humanities-educated self was mostly a cumulative process, with moments of awakening such as the one regarding history in Gordon Wood's course on the American Revolution. Courses in American poetry and literature contributed. So did the English course with the ingenious title "Sages and Satirists," for which I happily stayed up all night to write a paper on Thoreau and his sageness and sensibilities (having not given myself enough time to handwrite a draft, I had to type most of it from notes and scribblings and dogeared pages in Thoreau's work, accompanied by Fig Newtons, ice cream, and Ritz crackers on our kitchen table).

Professor Beiser's introductory political science course jarred my sensibilities, including feelings of trepidation and intimidation. In this I was not alone. The course attracted a horde of students, but Professor Beiser treated it as a small seminar just the same. Interrogation was one of his main pedagogical tools. We all shrunk and slunk in our lecture hall seats when he started class by calling out names randomly from the class list, demanding that one of us expound upon something in the readings—"Mr. ____, what does Hobbes mean when he talks about the pusillanimous nature of man?" With a question on something like pusillanimity you would be ashamed to slump in your seat, so we all followed the readings closely in that course.

It was in Professor Beiser's course, during my second semester at Brown, that I wrote a paper analyzing *The Autobiography of Malcom X* using the lens of "minorities rule," a concept developed by the political theorist Robert Dahl. The concept might sound abstract, but I found myself thoroughly committed to trying to understand Malcom X's life in terms of the suppression and empowerment of marginalized voices. Applying Dahl meant asking fundamental questions about whether our democratic system supports a minority or group of minorities in standing up for itself, whether equal rights and freedom for all made it imperative for minorities to be able to do so, and whether the majority is uplifted, too, when that happens. This paper was similar in experience to my paper for Brother James on "The Grand Inquisitor," written about a year earlier; but it was much more tightly written, directed at a political rather than a religious and spiritual question, and opened me to the value of using a theoretical concept as a lens to analyze and understand. The questions seemed so relevant and socially important, with Malcom X's assassination and the assassinations of Martin Luther King Jr. and Robert Kennedy, a strong advocate for civil rights, still fresh in the public mind.

Abraham Lincoln's question, enshrined in his Gettysburg address, whether "a new nation conceived in liberty, and dedicated to the proposition that all men are created equal . . . can long endure," was at the heart of what I learned about the history of civil rights and social movements. The evidence of great legal strides encoded in the Civil Rights Acts—notably the Act of 1866 establishing citizenship for "all persons" born in the United States, the Fourteenth and Fifteenth Amendments affirming voting rights, the Act of 1964 extending the prohibition of discrimination, and the Voting Rights Act of 1965 clearing away obstacles to the right to vote—reinforced what I wanted to believe about steady social progress and the arc of the moral universe. But my idealized version of our history gave way inexorably to a realistic understanding of the length of the arc and the extent of effort necessary to keep it on its course towards justice. My belief in the endeavor didn't waver; as much as I encountered the record of setback and challenge in our history, I found even more inspiration and reason for hope. What I needed at some point, however, was to see the endeavor in more personal terms, in a real human context. The world of public education that I was entering offered that context; it was (and is) a microcosm of so much of our democratic struggle, aspiration, and hope.

TEACHING, FAINTING, AND DEMOCRACY IN THE CLASSROOM

After my graduation from Brown, I began my second summer as an assistant camp director at Yawgoog, working with Bruce Ingham at Three Point. Bruce was a science teacher with a penchant for fastidious organization. My penchant was for camp programming, so we were a complementary pair.

Some years before I met him, Bruce had been an eighth grader in my father's social studies class. My father maintained a disciplined classroom and, on the face of it, you would think that would have suited Bruce just fine. But one day when it was his turn to stand in front of the class for an oral report, Bruce succumbed to nervousness and fainted. Bruce attributes his momentary slip from the normal view of his classmates more to Dad's strong presence than to any discomfort from being in front of the class. What strikes me is that the dad I knew and the teacher Bruce knew seemed to be two distinct people. Sure, Dad could dish out some tough love, but he had to reach a point of exasperation to do so, which didn't happen as often as it might have.

Dad as teacher, however, needed to draw on that part of his personality that would create the ethos for learning that he considered optimal. He often mentioned the importance of a certain "command presence" in the classroom; to whatever extent that meant projecting a no-nonsense demeanor, it was easy to imagine Dad doing it very well. As I knew from talking with him about his teaching, and from a visit to his classroom, he otherwise leaned into a more Socratic role, asking questions and challenging students and enjoying the give-and-take. As a postscript to Bruce's story, I should add that he went on to teach at the same school as Dad and had only respect for him. Whenever I saw Bruce at a Camp Yawgoog alumni reunion he would ask about Dad, and he was there at Dad's wake.

Every teacher is faced with the daunting task of creating a "Goldilocks zone" for learning—a "just-right" space for all their students to thrive; and every teacher must face some degree of struggle in the process. In my mind cultivating this space required establishing not so much a commanding presence in the classroom as a purposeful and authentic one. Students are experts at sniffing out inauthenticity and insincerity; they need to trust that the teacher is truly there for them and for their learning. Like any student teacher, I was concerned about getting my presence right. My purposefulness was serious and real, backed up by careful planning meant to draw students into meaningful engagement with interesting subject matter. I was sincere but had to avoid being too earnest. I felt ever ready to smile and respond to good effort, hoping that a positive approach would earn the cooperation if not the enthusiasm of students. I also focused on developing a sense of community conducive to trusted and honest exchange, mutual support, and collaboration.

I imagined an ethos and learning culture much like what I found so powerful at Yawgoog, in which young people would thrive. It took me a while to understand the challenge of developing this with each group, the time and steady nurturance it would take. I was encouraged during my student teaching at Toll Gate by the response I got to "The Great Rhode Island Road Race," an activity I developed for juniors and seniors in my Rhode Island history class. I provided pairs of students with road maps and instructions. To travel from one point to another on their maps, following the "Road Race" route, they had to complete various tasks that called upon knowledge and analysis of history and geography, covering everything from immigration to industrialization, using resources such as economic data and firsthand accounts that were located at different stations in the room. For the most part this activity generated the kind of unselfconscious immersion that I considered an important sign that things were going well; and that I also saw as a sign that formal learning and Yawgoog learning culture could merge to some extent. But schools are complicated places, with structures and practices that sometimes work at cross-purposes with their mission to educate all students and, as John Dewey and others believed, to serve as a lever of social progress and reform; and I had so much to learn.

Having finished student teaching and another summer at Yawgoog, in the fall of 1977 I took a couple of required courses in history, with my master's thesis on the horizon. I also took another step into my teaching career by accepting a short-term eight-week position at Aldrich Junior High School in Warwick, where my dad had once worked. It was there that I had a visceral collision between institutional structure and my nascent understanding of the democratic mission of schooling.

Like many if not most schools, Aldrich followed the conventional wisdom of tracking students. Tracking had (and has) a certain common-sense appeal—students should be placed at an academic level matched to their performance because that is where they will learn best. The companion notion is that curriculum can be adapted and paced more readily, too.

I first encountered tracking while in high school at La Salle, which divided core academic classes into three basic levels. There was enough flexibility at La Salle to place some students at more than one level based on their performance in particular subjects. Still, I noticed that some students mistook performance for ability and internalized the belief that they were less (or more) capable than others depending on their level. Later, more aware as an educator, I wondered whether and how expectations for students like me in the highest group were different from others, and so whether and how I might have benefited more.

The most generous interpretation of the benefits of tracking is that it will enable teachers to meet students where they are; education in this sense will be personalized. While meeting students where they are is a widely accepted maxim in teaching, it begs the question of who students are, especially those who are habitually in lower tracks compared to higher ones. Tracking also sidesteps a lot of other questions, such as what constitutes "ability" and whether students at different levels are all taught the great strength and potential of their minds. The most pernicious interpretation of tracking is that it prepares students for the work and stratum of society that suits them, what some call meritocracy and others "sorting." People on both sides of the tracking issue stake a claim for the democratic value of their position.

At Aldrich I felt like I was on a seesaw that teetered toward the pernicious interpretation, with very little to counterbalance it. Tracking was practiced with meticulous fidelity: students were grouped in at least a dozen levels. One of my seventh-grade classes purportedly was first, while one of my eighth-grade classes was last. The seventh-grade class admittedly was fun. The students approached anything I dreamed up with alacrity. Turn the classroom into a big grid to practice plotting latitude and longitude and they were all in. Distribute around the room a set of large black and white photos depicting various scenes from life in India, rummaged from a social studies storage room, and they were ready to interrogate them as cultural journalists and share the stories they learned. Such activities did entail a lot of movement and generated a lot of buzz; but what seemed energetic learning to me was countercultural in the school, and one day the principal stepped into my classroom disapprovingly. My eighth-grade class also generated a lot of movement, albeit for very different reasons, and no one ever visited it.

Unlike today, there were few resources back then designed to support students with various needs, teach social-emotional awareness and self-regulation, and address hidden trauma. A typical approach was to group students with disparate needs together; this practice harkened back to "ungraded" rooms from the turn of the century, something I learned while doing research on my master's thesis, which I focused on immigrants and education in Providence from 1900-1920. My eighth-grade group comprised twelve very different students, but it seemed like many more. Where one was peripatetic, another seemed perpetually distracted; where one would disappear in a flash, usually to be found hiding in the cloak closet, another needed careful handholding. Only rarely could I get their collective attention. I tried every stratagem I could think of, short of adopting the mien of a disgruntled ogre. I achieved a modicum of success by meeting with each student individually while they worked on what I hoped were meaningful worksheets, distributing my attention according to need; but the amount of my available attention was woefully inadequate. I tried a democratic process of determining class rules, linking it to the concept of a constitution, and the novelty of the idea that they could have a direct role in their own learning captivated them, but ever so briefly. Every day I came in feeling both determined and in danger of drowning; and wondered whether I was an imposter.

During my last day of teaching at the school, the eighth-grade class astounded and moved me by presenting me with a gift—a tie—something apparently organized by one of the bigger boys, who stood up and made the presentation with a shy smile. In that moment I learned what so many teachers learn: how easy it is to lose sight of students' full humanity in their struggle to adapt to what you (and their school) think is important for them to be doing. With the school adapting more to them, with help from a student support team, with greater expectations and a different grouping strategy, I can imagine these students feeling truly valued—and so learning to value school—and having the more enlivening educational experience they deserved.

The lesson I learned from the eighth-grade group had many variations and I benefited from the ones I experienced. A year or so later I was teaching a 9th grade "special" class; today it might be considered a moderate special needs class, although I can readily see the students included in more heterogeneous classes with personalized support. I planned for them variations of what I prepared for my other 9th grade class in ancient civilizations. But my plans were often less dazzling to them than they were to me. They were willing students, and so their blank stares in response to what I asked them to do finally disconcerted me enough that I had to pause for a deep rethink.

To that point I regularly created activities that put students in the middle of discussing, analyzing, evaluating, or creating; but as engaging as they might be, these ultimately were born of my sense of the subject matter and of beneficial learning. I realized that I was asking them to enter my thought process and conception, when I might have done more to enter theirs. I gradually learned how much I needed to be present to them and listen to their thoughts as capable and interesting young people; how much I needed to mold my teaching to them more than they needed to mold their learning process to me. Hard sometimes for teachers to do, I had to learn to de-center myself, to recognize teaching as a dynamic process of both igniting and responding to the minds, hearts, and voices of students, and appreciate students as an integral force in the curriculum.

I didn't abandon my Yawgoog vision of classroom teaching, but I became preoccupied with teaching's day-to-day demands and how to work effectively within the institution that is school. In the coming two years, I would have a highly engaging companion in this effort, a young teacher like me named Seth Kreisberg. I would also learn how much could be accomplished in the name of school outside the classroom by starting "B.S."—the "Before School" group. But that all happened after my cross-country trip with Bill Kenyon. And none of it would have happened if I hadn't met Cathy Clark.

MARDI GRAS AND BUFFALOES

With coursework complete and my master's thesis due at the end of the spring, I had some flexible time. Bill Kenyon, precocious kitchen manager and cook at camp and a big brother to the young staff who worked under his direction, told me at the annual Yawgoog staff reunion in December that he wanted to take some time off from his undergraduate work at the University of Rhode Island. We casually tossed around the idea of a cross-country road trip and then latched on to it. Somehow we both realized that this was one of those fortuitous moments in life that needed a spontaneous rather than calculated response.

In late January I arrived at Bill's family home in East Greenwich in the Datsun B210. We would start down the east coast, using our geographically scattered Yawgoog friends as guideposts and potential hosts, and take a tent to take advantage of low-cost camping opportunities. We would then head west along the Gulf coast to avoid complications from winter weather and keep going until our limited funds ran out. Our first leg brought us to Yawgoog friend Jeff Manickas in Washington, D.C., where he was engaged in some government-related work. After touring the major sites in D.C., we met friends of Bill's family in Atlanta, had a short stop at Disney World in Orlando, and stayed with my cousin Jimmy for a night in St. Petersburg on the way to Mardi Gras in New Orleans.

We camped outside New Orleans, entering the city until we ran into one of the Mardi Gras parades sponsored by a "Krewe." A Krewe is one of the social clubs responsible for the pageantry and sounds of Mardi Gras, including the beads and emblems and other baubles that flow freely from parade floats into your hands. We visited the French Quarter with its bars opening onto the streets, accompanied by the sounds of jazz and the clink of beer mugs. We had stepped into a citywide celebration, and it was raucous.

From New Orleans we made it to Houston where we stayed at a Motel 6. While watching the national news our attention was arrested by the report of a blizzard up north. It took a moment for us to realize that the reporter was waist-deep in snow in Rhode Island. We were missing the Blizzard of 1978 that paralyzed New England for days.

We traveled through New Mexico, were duly impressed by the voluminous bat guano at Carlsbad Caverns, and visited the pueblo at Taos before crossing the Sangre de Cristo Mountains into Colorado. There we stayed in a bunkhouse at Philmont Scout Ranch, hearing owls at night and glimpsing wild antelope during the day. In Denver we roomed with multitalented Yawgoog friend Kevin Bowling, who baked us fresh bread. We would make it to Las Vegas and Los Angeles and San Francisco before heading eastward again. Las Vegas blinded us with neon light; apart from putting a few quarters that we had from family members into slot machines (no luck), our most memorable activity was seeing John Travolta in the movie Saturday Night Fever. In San Franciso the Datsun needed a new alternator; thankfully we could stay with Jim Azzinaro, another Yawgoog friend. From San Francisco we started the long trek homeward, accelerated by our diminishing cash supply. I marked my twenty-third birthday in Winnemucca, Nevada.

Our encounter with buffaloes happened in Yellowstone National Park. It was the middle of winter, and the park was in a brilliantly pristine state, with virtually no tourists in sight. A thick blanket of snow made the roads impassable except by snowshoe, ski, or snowmobile. We rented snowmobiles, transfixed by elk at the edges of the glittering Yellowstone River and buffaloes pawing the snow near hot springs in search of sustenance, snorting misty plumes of air. We moved slowly, pausing often.

As we turned into a blind curve, what had been a dreamy aesthetic experience suddenly changed tenor. We were confronted by a group of about a dozen buffaloes only forty yards or so away; they were as surprised as we were and as wary. The large bulls immediately stood between us and the smaller cows who slowly trudged through the snow. Mesmerized by the scene, I produced my 35-millimeter Pentax K-1000 and readied it to take a photo; but alas, I had no more photos left on the roll. While I struggled with the camera in the cold, the bulls took steps towards us. Bill was decisive: he circumvented the small herd, trusting his snowmobile in a field of snow too deep for the buffaloes to maneuver. It took me a moment to see the wisdom of Bill's action, a process accelerated by the sight of those glaring shaggy and snow-speckled heads. I followed Bill's trail while lamenting the lost opportunity for an epic photograph.

CATHY AND A PIVOTAL CROSSROAD

Lost opportunity. Sometimes we know there is opportunity, yet we don't know how to seize it or are restrained by some complicated feeling that is hard to name. Sometimes we don't know that opportunity is in front of us because seeing it would mean a depth of self-honesty that we are afraid to plumb and/or a judgment that we are too inexperienced to make. The variations are endless; the one constant is loss. When it involves love we can only hope that the loss is so poignant that we learn from its every tearful pore.

After returning from our cross-country adventure in early March, I turned my attention in earnest to my thesis and to a teaching opportunity back at Toll Gate High School, where I would stay through the end of the school year. On the surface, I was sailing on familiar waters. I had to meet several challenges: entice students into a debate on Truman's decision to drop the innocuous sounding "Little Boy" and "Fat Man" on Hiroshima and Nagasaki; prepare for my first year as camp director of Three Point; and get the thesis done. Below the surface? I was plumbing unknown depths.

There were several Master of Arts in Teaching students from Brown teaching at Toll Gate in the spring. With our common interest in exploring the complexities of teaching and trading curriculum ideas, and with me practically a veteran in their eyes from my prior experience with Mr. Olson and the school, we connected readily. But "we" soon became Cathy Clark and me. Cathy made conversation easy and natural. She was affable, with a soft engaging and sometimes winking smile, and curious in a genuine and unobtrusive way. She was quick to understand, and as ready to reflect as to laugh. She seemed comfortable with herself, but I sensed that she also had learned a lot about herself to get to that point. Her casual demeanor belied her active and thoughtful mind.

If I had any uncertainty about whether we had crossed the line between professional and friend and perhaps something more, Cathy put that question to rest. Apparently knowing her own feelings far better than I did mine, she pulled me into her classroom after school one day, shut the door, and before either of us could think any more about it promptly gave me a sweet kiss. She told me that she had been wanting to do that, as if it were the most natural thing in the world. And indeed, mirabile dictu, it sure felt that way.

But what did the kiss mean? I was troubled because Cathy had told me she was engaged to a guy studying at McGill University in Montreal. We had reached an ambiguous moment that neither of us was inclined to address. We continued to meet as usual and for longer periods, venturing outside of the school environment for ice cream and a trip to the beach to check out a place at which my brothers were staying, all the while avoiding the question of what our togetherness meant, as if by doing so we could protect our small tender space.

But camp was looming fast, just as the transition from Brown was for Cathy. As school ended, I left for camp convinced that we were at an impasse in our relationship, and stifling any alternative thoughts. I also left with little means of communication. Except for a phone at the Bucklin administration building, phones at camp were for internal use. With the ubiquity of cell phones today, it is hard to imagine being so unconnected and with such little recourse. Suddenly life for Cathy and me was tantamount to living on two separate islands.

It was staff training week at camp, and my days were full until I went to the cabin where I was staying. One evening, the night still and contemplative, the roar of a Volkswagen beetle broke the silence, and I knew it was Cathy. She had driven almost forty miles from Providence, spurred by her roommate telling her that she had no choice but to go see me.

We sat close, happy to be together, but sure of nothing else. Cathy might have felt the weight of ambivalence and hoped for a breakthrough of clarity by seeing me. She might have hoped that I would make the breakthrough, give her a sign that would give her the courage to chart a new direction. I was not helpful; I thought I was taking some kind of moral stance out of respect for her engagement. But the truth was that I didn't know how to listen to my heart or know the power of the heart to overcome circumstances such as these, and I was fearful of taking steps that I hadn't taken before. True to her character, Cathy didn't press me; perhaps she felt too conflicted herself to do so. In the short term we were on two different roads, and the longer we stayed on them the harder it would be to change course. And that's basically what happened.

I had never felt homesick at camp; this was the first time I felt alone and adrift.

Although Cathy and I would have precious little opportunity to reconnect, the immediate stretch of road I was traveling was all due to her, and it would prove another formative experience. She had encouraged me to apply for a history teaching position at her high school in New Canaan, where she had a close relationship with Bob Gardner, the head of the history department, a thoughtful and considerate man who had supported her as a student. Bob and I would co-coach the first mock trial team at the school several years later, also the first Connecticut state champs, a distinction achieved after the students hung tough in a trial before a judge in a Hartford courthouse. After I accepted an offer to teach there, Cathy pledged to help me find somewhere to live.

SETH AND THE ILLUSIONS OF THE PROMISED LAND

Seth Kreisberg and I met by happenstance, providentially I might add. We both had been hired by New Canaan, Seth to teach English. As part of my day trip to New Canaan to get oriented, I went to the school. Outside the principal's office I saw Seth, intermittently looking around and overlooking me because, at six feet, six inches tall, I was not immediately in his line of vision. Seth was supposed to meet a prospective housemate who failed to show. He offered to introduce me to the apartment he and his partner Irma Gonzalez had lined up; Irma would teach middle school Spanish in nearby Darien. With Cathy's gentle encouragement, and with rental spaces in short supply, I agreed to the arrangement. I would live with Seth and Irma for six of the next eight years, two in New Canaan, and the last four in Somerville, Massachusetts, on Electric Avenue.

New Canaan began a geographical shift in my life, unmooring me from Providence. Being with Seth and Irma accentuated the shift because of their backgrounds—Seth from White Plains, NY, Irma from Florida, her parents from Cuba—and because of their social perspectives. Seth, keen to address issues of class and power, would challenge my educational thinking, as I like to think I did his. But despite its intimation of a promised land, I viewed New Canaan as more an outpost in my life than a new center. Physically I was still closely tied to Rhode Island; year-round planning for summers at Camp Yawgoog still formed the rhythmic pattern of my life. Providence was bred into me; wherever I went I was simply a homing pigeon, ready to return.

I met Irma—more accurately, Irma bounded into view—when I was moving in. Raven-haired, long-legged and lanky, with an engulfing smile, Irma greeted me warmly. As I would learn, she was forthright and honest, and convincing with logic she shared liberally, with no need to resort to any of Aristotle's fallacies and quite up to the task of exposing your own. She combined sensitivity with sharp perceptiveness. Irma was one of the friendliest and keenest-eyed women I had met; her example was powerful for me.

It was easy to see why Seth and Irma were together, both strong in conviction, socially aware, friendly, and forthright. Seth played basketball at Wesleyan University, and we connected on the court. I learned quickly to pass it to him in a high-post position just above the foul line, trusting in his court vision and his own readiness to pass to make a good play. He was a good teammate, holding you accountable no less than himself. We played together in the faculty-student game at New Canaan. We would later help our team at the Harvard Graduate School of Education beat the Divinity School for the grad-school championship, which we appreciated as a sign of divine neutrality in the field of sport.

Seth impressed me with his determination to unlock the minds of all kids and engage them in critical social thinking through literature, and by his willingness to challenge institutional convention. Faced with a group of students who had been scuffling through school, a group that he viewed as handicapped by low expectations, he tried a different tack. Rather than ask them to explain what they visualized in the novel they were reading, he asked them to depict it. The students responded enthusiastically, constructing three-dimensional versions of the setting as they saw it. Viewing their interpretations and efforts as worthy in themselves, and any effort to dissect them as inhumane, he gave all the students a "100" for their numerical quarter grades. I don't remember whether he had to justify this action to the administration; in any case, the grades stood.

During our second year together, Seth and I seized the opportunity to team-teach a two-hour "American Studies" course for juniors. We hunkered down often for late-night planning sessions, sometimes beginning with "What are we going to do?" and navigating Seth's interjections of "Why?" We built joint rationales from our different starting points and were willing to try different modes of learning and activities; it was a strenuous but powerful learning process for both of us. The late sessions were not optimal for an early riser and runner like me; but they were the only way for us to keep up with the demands of our individual and joint work.

The following year Seth and Irma went to pursue master's degrees at Harvard, Seth at the school of education, Irma at the divinity school. I would continue in New Canaan, by this time working as much with students outside as inside the classroom. Apart from the mock trial team and two faculty-student plays, my activity included the "Before School" ("B.S.") program, which I started in my first year, and living at "A Better Chance," aka the "ABC House." Both activities taught me in personal terms, the terms that matter most, the complexities of the school and the challenges facing education as a democratic institution. And quite unexpectedly, at ABC House I was introduced to Thomas Merton.

"B.S."

In flouting the conventional grading policy at New Canaan, Seth was making a broader philosophical statement regarding the whole culture of competition at the school. New Canann was a community of wealthy high-achieving people with similar expectations for its children, and an underlying and unquestioned faith in the fairness and virtue of meritocracy, of everyone getting what they earned. At its best, the culture drew out the best in students; but it could also lead to petty games of one-upmanship. It bore down heavily on some students—some sought means to escape, some simply disengaged, some felt disconnected and lonely. The school aspired to be a community that fostered excellence for all but could not dissolve the hierarchies and self-imposed status differentiations that infiltrated student life.

As in many schools, the values of opportunity, individualism, competition, and community struggled to harmonize in New Canaan; they were like musical notes on the same scale but not always in the same key. I felt the dissonance with my Yawgoog educational experience, where the community supported everyone's individual effort, and competition, when it occurred, usually allied with teamwork. But Yawgoog was simple and self-contained compared to the learning environment of schools like New Canaan High, where complicated and unresolved tensions in society found ways of seeping in. Seth and his students stepped momentarily outside the prevailing culture; motivated by my desire for a more communal ethos, I ventured outside, too.

In the middle of my first year of teaching at New Canaan, not at all sure of the response I would get, I casually explained my interest in forming a "before-school" group to the sophomores in my class on modern European history, alluding to activities like team-building games and the opportunity to start the day on a bright and uplifting note. A few students looked at friends to gauge how this registered on the "maybe-cool-to-try" scale. A couple of hands went up, and then a couple more, forming what for the next two and one-half years would be the core group of Chris and Carlin and Kirsti and Ann and Janet and Shawn. They would be joined by many others, with at least several dozen participating for some length of time.

Yes, we called our "Before-School" group "B.S.," a tongue-in-cheek way for us to announce our iconoclastic identity vis-à-vis other school clubs. B.S. indeed was different, an alternative especially for students looking for a group unburdened by particular social expectations and their attendant peer pressures or prerequisite skills. In a sense it was an alter ego for the school.

Somewhat to my surprise, the kids showed up with me at the gym at 6:15 a.m. and kept coming three times a week. I would hear a grumble now and then—"Do you realize how early I had to get up to get my hair ready?!?"—which I took as a message of self-sacrifice for a greater good. Joining and attending was a matter of personal willingness and otherwise a commitment to our unwritten group norms regarding healthy and respectful group play, acceptance, inclusion, and teamwork, and support for anyone stretching beyond their comfort zone to try out new activities. A brilliant orange rising sun, silk-screened by Chris Briggs on our yellow t-shirts, was our symbol, "grow in mind, body, and spirit" our informal slogan. Activities might include any team-oriented initiative game that I sanguinely introduced as well as more conventional ones such as ultimate frisbee and street hockey. The sound of "score!" would reverberate frequently during the latter, especially after Steve Gyde and Joel Keffer joined the group, accompanied by idiosyncratic forms of dance and self-congratulation.

The "human knot" became our signature activity. We would try regularly to break our record for the number of us we could disentangle after interlocking hands randomly across the circle we formed. Cries of accomplishment accompanied every successful unraveling and the restoration of our original circle. Everyone was welcome into the knot, as they were in the group. I usually offered up an edifying quotation to conclude our hour or so together, which sometimes elicited a thoughtful silence rather than silent eye-rolling, with all invited to add any reflection. We emerged afterwards into the school corridors mostly alert and alive, an incomprehensible state in the dim view of others groping their way to their classrooms. As the group matured, I had less to do by way of group management. Senior group members quietly reinforced our commitment to positive well-being, as well as an ethic of respect and acceptance; that is, all except Carlin, who reinforced it with more vocal fervor and volume than others.

B.S. was at least as nourishing for me as for the students, and the closest I came to reproducing the spirit of Yawgoog in school. To leave nothing to chance in this regard, we went directly to Yawgoog for weekend camping trips several times. I confess to a bout of concern during our first campout when Chris awkwardly tried to manage a wood fire for cooking; but I would learn that this was merely a sign of a willing and generous spirit. Chris would not only survive but prove incredibly resourceful and dedicated. He was our design master for logos and other creative work, foreshadowing his college and career path. Chris and Carlin developed a friendship that would grow into a deeper relationship after they graduated. About three decades later Carlin visited me with her son, a young man who reminded me instantly of his dad. Recalling our time together in B.S., I mentioned how "good" it was; Carlin quickly corrected me—"It was much better than good."

Feeling a need to mediate between New Canaan speech and the foreign intonations and stresses of Rhode Island speech, Naomi Schiffman took it upon herself to compose "Rhode Islandese: A Very Abridged Dictionary of the Rhode Island Dialect." Only a sophomore, Naomi was a quiet yet diligent and astute observer and, apparently, a budding linguistic anthropologist (Naomi's study of linguistics was short-lived—she became a pediatric cardiologist). A small booklet, "Rhode Islandese" is full of Naomi's fine and neat script, as well as phonetic spellings that mimic the tendency of native Bostonians and other New Englanders to drop the "r" sound at the end of words. Naomi captures some unique expressions that Rhode Islanders will instantly recognize, especially if they are from Providence. And she provides illustrative sentences drawing mainly on the foibles of B.S.'ers on Yawgoog camping trips. Here are a few excerpts from her dictionary:

Befoah—earlier; previously. People should make sure that their site is level befoah laying down their sleeping bag, just in case it rains.

Bubblah—a device with a small jet of water suitable for drinking. Only in Rhode Island can you find real bubblahs to drink from.

Feeah—a feeling of alarm or fright; terror; dread. Janet conquered her feeahs and went rappelling.

Fiyah—a chemical reaction releasing light and heat. Carlin was confused until Tom told her that a green stick can't catch on fiyah.

Gawht—past tense of get. The Menu Committee gawht a lot of good food; unfortunately, they left it all at home.

Tawk—to use human speech; articulate words. We know how to tawk here in Connecticut.

Yooz—people addressed by the speaker. One of these days yooz guys will get the radio skit right.

At Yawgoog, in addition to hiking, cooking whatever the menu committee had set for the menu (provided that the committee had packed the food they "gawht"—they had to make an emergency run to a local supermarket the one time they discovered, with nervous astonishment, they had not), and trying out team-oriented elements of the developing ropes course, we would organize activities for a middle school group run by Al Mink, a principal who also was a senior leader on the camp staff. This experience fortified our confidence in planning and running a schoolwide team-based activity back at New Canaan high school, which rotated teams of six-eight students through a variety of team-based initiatives and tasks. Our most ambitious trip by far was to England to visit one of the girls from our group whose family had moved there. Scheduled around the February vacation in 1981, the trip coincided with the graduation year of the core members who paved the way more than two years before, and most of them went. We sold candy canes during the holiday season to defray the costs. My sister Kathy joined as an older female presence (except when she slipped over the English Channel on a twenty-four-hour jaunt to visit Paris), rounding out our group of thirteen.

Yawgoog played a significant role in the England trip as well. The previous summer a reporter for the British Broadcasting Corporation had covered Great Britain's entry in the America's Cup sailing races in Newport. Searching for a substitute gig when the Brits bowed out, and involved in Cub Scouts back home, John visited us at Yawgoog. I didn't forget his generous offer to help any of us who might make it to England and frankly took advantage of it. He was generous to a fault, arranging to pick us up at the airport in classic London taxis, hosting us in Winchester in a small place that we made into a patchwork quilt with our sleeping bags, and guiding us to Stonehenge and a "ploughman's lunch" of bread and cheese at a nearby pub. We bestowed upon him honorary membership in the form of one of our newly branded "B.S. Abroad" t-shirts and a sweatshirt with our signature sunrise logo.

CAMP, THE MALE BASTION, AND THE LOST CAR FEINT

Taking the B.S. group on camping trips to Yawgoog broke through the male exclusiveness of camp and showed me firsthand the value of an inclusive group experience. But the prospect of integrating girls and young women into camp as I knew it seemed remote.

There was a strong analogy between my experience at La Salle and at Yawgoog insofar as girls were concerned, reinforcing and extending my reticence through the entire year. Yawgoog in this regard reflected the Boy Scout movement overall. The presence of women in the Boys Scouts was not entirely unprecedented—young women were able to participate in the "Explorer" program for older youth as early as 1969. Otherwise, the Boy Scouts of America, now Scouting America, was a male-dominated domain. This exclusiveness always made me a little uneasy when I saw the enthusiasm that my sister and, later, my daughter had for the camp experience that my brothers and I lived and breathed.

In our day, a woman in camp was a rare occurrence, so rare that rumor of an appearance spread like wildfire though the staff. Some rumors were started by staff members who used the binoculars on waterfront watch towers to look for signs of the resident doctor's daughters on the small beach fronting the doctor's cabin on the north side of the pond. Older staff sometimes interrogated their younger brethren about whether they had any female siblings and, if so, whether they were old enough to drive to camp to pick up their brothers for their weekly days off. Women were not permitted beyond the Bucklin building except to go to the amphitheater for the Saturday Night Show, so the rendezvous point for a pick-up was usually the camp parking lot near the ranger's station.

That's where I found myself in my friend John Carty's well-traveled car one Saturday night with the older sister of one of our kitchen boys. The Saturday Night Show took place in the J. Harold Williams Amphitheater, complete with footlights and a spotlight that roved over a raised grassy stage flanked by two totem poles representing Chief Williams and camp lore, and families and friends were welcome. The show had just ended, and Jimmy D's sister had attended, watching me lead the Camp Three Point song and cheer as well as perform in a skit dressed as a woman. The two of us had yet to meet and I wondered whether my thespian performance might have led her to question her judgment about meeting at all. She might have had some kind of advanced billing because John had set it up. In any case she apparently was more intrigued than discouraged.

John and his car figure prominently in this story. First, the car. It was mechanically capable of getting him here and there, especially to his favorite watering hole, "Twin Willows" on Boston Neck Road in Narragansett. But it lacked aesthetic appeal. What looked like stripes from a distance became striations of rust up close. If you imagined John's car as an archaeological dig—something easy to do—you were sure to find artifacts from his imbibing experiences.

John had never been a Scout but enjoyed the company of camp guys like Hop and me and Kevin Bowling, whom he met at Providence College, and who introduced him to us. An aspiring teacher and sports coach, John also enjoyed working with young people, so we recruited him to work with us at camp. He spent a few summers working with us while studying history and preparing to follow his vocation at the Rhode Island School for the Deaf. Hop and I convinced him to help us run Troop 6 North Providence as well, which we did together for a few years, starting when we were still in college. Soon after, he was awarded the "Pelican" medal by the Providence Catholic diocese for his service to Scouting. This recognition mystified Hop and me, considering that John had spent so little time in Scouting. It turns out that a priest concerned for John's best interests talked with him at a PC hockey game and decided that he would benefit from this recognition.

Pelicans, we learned, can be extraordinarily self-giving, inspiring the award; a pelican will pluck meat from its own breast to feed its young if necessary. There is an image of a pelican doing just that on the ceiling of St. Pius Church on Eaton Street, right across from Providence College, which John attended his whole life. John became "the Pelican" to us, and the three of us became "the Pelicans" when Hop and I were given the same award a year later. Whenever we parted, we would put our hands together and proclaim our ironic Pelican slogan, proposed by John—"One for all, all for one, and every Pelican for himself!"—and raise our hands with a flourish.

Hop, John, and I had several memorable adventures and misadventures on land and water during those final years of the 1970s, enough to sustain our storytelling for the rest of our lives. Most involved canoes, including one trip on the Moosup River after most of the snow from the Blizzard of '78 had melted, with the river gushing. Hop and I were in the lead canoe, John and my brother Rob in the other, which we borrowed from the father of two of our Scouts. While navigating a narrow curve, with water careening over a fallen tree, John and Rob tipped, and their canoe became wedged against a submerged branch, with part of it puncturing the hull. John and Rob emerged shivering but unscathed. We had to call in Hop's father, the man who kept the machines at the Cranston Print Works running smoothly, to help us extricate the stricken canoe. We waited for him while trying to warm ourselves with a makeshift fire. Clifton's disappointment in us was palpable as he silently rigged a double pulley and hoisted out the damaged craft, with Hop maneuvering it in the water in his skivvies.

Then there was the February campout on Curtis Tract at Yawgoog, where we took our troop late on a Friday afternoon for a district camporee, only to discover that we were the only troop willing to brave the penetrating cold, with temps in the low single digits. We pitched our canvas pup tents with the ceilings dropped low and newspaper padding our ground cloths for insulation, and gathered firewood as daylight quickly waned. We built a huge fire, cooked hot dogs, and then, necessity overcoming scruple, used the hot dog water to make hot chocolate. No one complained, especially when we added slices of warm homemade raisin bread provided by David Colannino's mom.

John's skill with watercraft improved. He later spent years plying the waters of Narragansett Bay in his beloved sailboat. We joined him occasionally, thankfully without incident.

Following my first year of teaching in New Canaan, and a year or so removed from my short-lived relationship with Cathy Clark, John coaxed and prodded me to consider dating, offering to lend his considerable expertise to the mission (I was still relatively shy as well as happily immersed in camp). He took responsibility for identifying prospective siblings of staff members, and thus Erin and I found ourselves in his car after a Saturday Night Show, together with a gaggle of empty beer bottles at our feet. John's car wasn't part of the plan, but my faithful Datsun B-210, parked under pine trees dripping from an afternoon shower, had failed to start due to a wet carburetor and despite the diligent application of hot air from a hair dryer located somehow by John.

I drove us gingerly in John's car to a place in Westerly recommended by some of the guys. We sat down and started a conversation when John and some of my other camp friends arrived. They tried to be discreet, but their curiosity overcame their sensitivity to the delicate stage in our relational process, and they came over to say hello and ask how we were doing.

Erin and I left first. That's when my imagined script for the night again went astray. In the parking lot, which was sizable, we looked vainly for John's car. I traced and retraced our route into the lot, to no avail. Even though awkwardness had become the norm for the night, I was worried. When John joined us, I shared the dilemma, to his apparent dismay. Then I suggested that we try a "lost car drill," and started spacing us apart by an arm's length, just as we would do in a "lost boy drill" at camp. Seeing my desperation, John put his arm around my shoulder and explained the ruse. He told me that his car was safe because he had moved it himself around the side of the building, using his backup key. I looked at him perplexed, trying to see the humor. Then he explained that he had moved it to deflect attention from the real issue, which was that my car, which he had revived and borrowed, had a new hole in the muffler, installed when John backed the car over a rock on his way out of camp.

I was powerless against the staccato roar of the muffler. Conversation on the ride back to camp amounted to tired smiles, nods, and headshaking. Erin agreed nonetheless to go out again, and we dated a few more times, albeit well clear of the environs of camp. My brother Rob had a much different experience from mine dating a staff man's sister. He and Peggy Ryan married and have three wonderful sons, two of whom became Eagle Scouts in Troop 1 Kingston, one of whom worked as a waterfront director at camp, following in the footsteps of his dad.

In 2019, beset by declining numbers and sex abuse lawsuits, Scouting rebranded itself, welcoming girls as members. A growing number of women now work alongside men at camp. In August 2024, Yawgoog celebrated the centenary of the oldest of its three camps, Camp Three Point. Having worked at Three Point for a decade, including six years as the director, I was invited to speak. Afterwards I met Peri, a young woman on the staff who worked in the nature program and who had contacted me by email regarding the history of the challenge program (The challenge program comprises different activities incorporating low and high ropes course elements, a climbing wall, and problem-solving, team-building initiatives). She was full of enthusiasm for her job, for the camp experience, and for Yawgoog's history and traditions. She reminded me of many of the staff with whom I had worked. As I write, Hannah, past director of the challenge program, has taken her turn as camp director of Three Point. Thinking of Peri and Hannah reminds me wistfully of my sister, who still can recite parts of the "radio" skit, and my daughter, who enjoyed practicing the "Captain, Captain, Captain!" skit with me as a young girl. I should mention my wife also, who sometimes hums "I like the mountains, I like the daffodils" and the chorus to "The Cat Came Back," old camp songs. The fact is that the women in my life and the lives of my friends have had to endure camp tales, obscure references to camp people and places, spontaneous eruptions of camp songs, and nostalgic reminiscences ever since they've known us.

This is not to say that the integration of women into camp has been simple. For one thing, the whole latrine system had to change. Where once we had "two-hole" and "three-hole" latrines—the holes side-by-side along a long plank—there are now separate facilities and flush toilets. Whether apocryphal or not, latrine stories involving such activities as fishing out a dollar bill are no doubt slipping out of memory and camp lore. But who can forget Rangers Al Gunther or Paul Forbes astride the "honey wagon," angling to pump out a latrine camouflaged by rhododendrons in the lee of a campsite? Not to mention Dave Kenyon, a taciturn and reliable man from Hope Valley renowned for his faded overalls (he was ahead of the curve, fashion-wise) and for uttering "Uh, yup" in response to any question, and who could find any water valve in camp as if he were a human divining rod.

Al Gunther, as wedded to camp as anyone, had his own mystique. He didn't suffer fools lightly, at least his idea of fools. Once, a Scout lodged himself in a tree like a modern young stylite or scared kitten, his way of drawing attention to his homesickness and desire to go home. One by one different staff offered soothing words and tried-and-true camp logic to coax him down ("We've all been homesick . . . how about we go to the crafts center together . . . think of how proud your parents will be when they see you awarded with a merit badge!"). This went on for the better part of the day. Tired of the soft-power approach, Al arrived with tough love and a chain saw, revved it up, and gave the Scout two options. Ah well, suffice it to say that new personalities, routines, and norms are now woven into camp life and tradition, even if the spirit of camp remains the same.

ABC HOUSE

Several B.S. members resided in the ABC House in New Canaan, two of whom would join us on the England trip. I had been one of the resident tutors since the beginning of the school year and knew the boys well.

My view of the ABC program was simple and idealistic. I judged it mainly on its purpose, reflected in its name ("A Better Chance"), to provide students with an opportunity to attend a high school more likely than their schools back home to qualify them for entrance to a major university. This opportunity would level the educational playing field for these students, wouldn't it? They deserved it, didn't they?

Eight boys lived at the ABC house, spanning ninth through twelfth grade, together with three adults. Two of us adults were teachers, although

I was the only one who taught at New Canaan High, where all the boys attended school. The boys were Black and Hispanic, the adults white, with different ethnic heritages. Home for the boys included New York City, Washington, D.C., and Memphis. They grew up in different social and cultural environments and attended underserved schools. Their personalities varied—among them, an older boy who appeared aloof but who kept his circle of trust small; a younger student with a big shy smile who hesitated thoughtfully before he spoke and a rambunctious fellow student who did not; two quiet studious boys, one seemingly more at ease and self-assured than the other, both with much more to say than their demeanors might suggest. They had been identified as candidates for the program by teachers and guidance counselors who hoped their participation would set them on a life trajectory better than the one typically taken by youth in their communities.

Our director was Steve Blumenthal, who taught English in a middle school in another town. With rimless glasses and the air of a scholar, Steve spoke softly but was firm and clear on matters concerning our little community and much else. One day he surprised me by handing me a book—"I thought you might like this"—that he had read in a course on spiritual autobiography. It was one of those mysterious moments in which you discover or see more clearly something about yourself by how someone sees you; a moment that affirms who you are and reminds you of what we can be and do for each other.

Steve had given me *The Seven Storey Mountain* by Thomas Merton and strangely, given my Catholic education, I had not come across it before. Steve was right—I liked it, drawn in by Merton's account of his upbringing, which took place largely in France and England and with his grandparents on Long Island, his struggle to find his bearings when he lost his mom at a young age and then his father as a teenager, his alienation from the dehumanizing forces he detected in a world careening towards World War II, his gradual intellectual and then heart-and-soul conversion to Catholicism, and his ultimate decision to give "all" to God by entering Gethsemani Abbey, a monastery of the Cistercian order in Kentucky, and committing to a life of solitude and contemplation. Merton's questions regarding the meaning of our existence, the reality and presence of God in the world and the importance of being aware of it, and whether and how to find yourself in God resonated with me, and in his journey I found a resource for my own.

I would follow Merton's journey—what he called the interior journey— through his writings and learn how he slowly transformed from the person of *The Seven Storey Mountain* who thought he had escaped from a broken world to a person, who happened to be a monk, who felt a compassionate solidarity with everyone in it. In seeking God in contemplative silence and solitude Merton paradoxically discovered love that embraced him and everyone else.

My deep response to *The Seven Storey Mountain* probably had something to do with an underlying sense of imbalance in my life. As much as I felt commitment and value in all that I was doing, my cup was overflowing more than I realized. There was a cumulative effect from my increasing responsibility and continuous involvement in school and camp. In my typical response to push ahead, I was neglecting the importance of room to breathe. In any event, my Merton immersion had begun, and Merton's writings and insight have been close companions ever since.

Each of the boys at ABC House had a local host family with whom they would stay monthly for a weekend of activities. The idea was to provide a home-like environment of support. The host families were chosen carefully. They were sincerely dedicated to their role and to varying degrees the boys felt their personal support; even if the home settings felt strange; conflict was rare.

The ABC House itself was an anomaly in the town, a languishing dull-gray, two-story construction. It stood off the main street lined with boutique shops and small businesses that extended to the train stop linking commuters to New York City. Few families lived nearby; most lived hidden from view in wooded estates at the end of long winding drives.

In its shabby and nondescript décor, the interior of the house matched the exterior. The kitchen was spare, with an old linoleum floor, wooden cupboards painted white, a large breadbox and fruit bowl on a moveable stand, and a banged-up and scarred gas stove likely to have surpassed its life expectancy. Still, weekday dinners were plentiful, thanks to a part-time cook without whom we all might have slowly perished from a snack-filled diet. Dinners were held in the adjacent dining room, which converted to a study space in the early evenings. There was another more open lounging space on the ground floor, together with a small and large bedroom. The boys and an adult slept upstairs.

One Saturday we took the boys to a movie. We returned to the darkened house via the kitchen back door. As soon as the light turned on, the boys swarmed to the nearest available food, which happened to be on the stand with the bread box. But they were brought up short by a rodent swarm that had arrived before them. Depending on whom you ask, the rodents were rats or mice. The distinction didn't matter to the boys, a few of whom had extensive experience with rodent extermination. They scattered the pack with brooms and whatever else was at hand, chasing down individual infiltrators. They were literally playing "Whac-A-Mole," and it was a spirited if short-lived affair.

The cook of course refused to enter the kitchen unless and until the extermination that the boys had begun was completed. In truth, this was an overdue task, as signs of rodents had been proliferating. Too often I woke in the night in my first-floor bedroom to gnawing and scratching sounds, thinking the walls were alive. I kept my hefty hiking boots within arm's reach, hoping they would intimidate, and threw them in the general direction of the sounds a few times. But the rodents were stealthy critters and rarely made an appearance. They miscalculated on movie night. The extermination job got done; but we had to replace the cook.

The ABC boys were at New Canaan High precisely for the chance it afforded to make it to an Ivy League or similar institution. Left unquestioned or unsaid was why they had to travel this pathway, why there were not others. Also left unquestioned was what it would mean for them to travel this pathway; what it would mean to try to thrive in a competitive and socially and culturally strange environment. The boys themselves didn't explicitly question their direction of travel and neither did I. We accepted along with others that a meritocratic pathway, even if paved with unequal opportunity and privilege and power, was the way to go. This was their chance.

Notwithstanding my general conformity with the prevailing ABC narrative, I felt uneasy when the boys struggled and I struggled to help them. The most disturbing moment for me occurred when one of the high school juniors appeared sweating profusely from anxiety. He was a highly motivated young man determined to qualify for an Ivy League school; this was his main measure of success. He placed relentless pressure on himself to excel academically; anything less was failure, not only for himself, but also for his community back home.

Representing their families and communities was one of the biggest burdens carried by the boys. They were living a terrible irony: to succeed for themselves they had to leave their communities; to the extent they did succeed, they also could be viewed as selling out. Facing that tension, they were left to question who they were and where they belonged. One of the boys told me going home was challenging because he felt estranged.

The experience of the ABC boys and the questions it raised became an important touchstone for my own efforts in education. These were capable young men asked to measure up to the work of students who had been groomed to measure up their whole lives. They were put on the starting line of a race that began way before they met their new classmates. They were asked to adapt to a culture that was built on privilege, which assumed that opportunity to be in a privileged meritocracy amounted to equity and a way to the American dream. What the boys experienced, what they could not fully voice, was the dissonance of educational, economic, and racial inequities, the heavy and unfair burden of a flawed system.

It is hard to apprehend let alone comprehend the system of which you are a part, even a system with the jarring contrasts experienced by the ABC boys, even when you're stressed by it. You may be less likely to surface from your submersion if you are surrounded by good and encouraging intentions, and when the myths buttressing those intentions are strong. I can tell you that the boy whose anxiety brought him close to a breaking point kept going and was accepted into an Ivy League college. He beat the odds, mostly by dint of extraordinary personal effort. Unfortunately, I don't know whether he went on to fulfill the ABC vision of a pipeline for future leaders from underrepresented groups. I wonder whether he and his ABC peers came to question the world governing the path they were put on, and whether they questioned the world they were being led to uphold. If they did, then they were in tune with one of the purposes of education in a democracy, as James Baldwin put it forcefully in a talk to teachers in 1963: "The paradox of education is precisely this—that as one begins to become conscious one begins to examine the society in which [one] is being educated . . . to examine society and try to change it and to fight it—at no matter what risk. This is the only hope society has."

HEIGHT, BLIGHT, AND MYSTICS

Barely dawn on a Sunday morning, while crossing the George Washington Bridge, with Manhattan like a mysterious shadowy world off to the right, I heard a metallic grinding noise that sounded like the Datsun was readying to fire an undercarriage missile in James Bond fashion. Alarmed, I pumped the brakes, until I realized that the driveshaft had chosen that moment to disengage and cease its vital function. Thankfully it was early and it was a Sunday, with almost no traffic on a bridge that converted to a parking lot during rush hour.

I found myself on the gentle downward slope of the bridge close to its juncture with land. I ventured outside the car, dazed and at a loss (still no cell phones). After a minute or so, a car paused at the end of a nearby on-ramp to survey the situation, a window rolled down, and a male voice hailed forth: "Hey, man, you need help?" When I explained my plight, the response was, "You need to go to Joe's," and a back seat door opened. The car was packed with a group of guys who appeared to be on the tail end of a long night of activity, so I thought it was a generous offer. I squeezed in and was escorted to "Joe's," a garage with towing services.

The towing guy drove the wrong way up the bridge to get to the car, ho-hum. When we returned, he went back to his chair, letting me know that the garage would be open the next morning. Delivered in the same ho-hum vein, this announcement flummoxed me: right place, bad timing. My senses blurred by my sleepless night and disoriented by the shift from a rugged natural landscape to a dreary urban one, I could only think of where I might find a haven at 7:30 in the morning. It was Sunday, so I asked if there was a church nearby, hoping that I might experience some form of enlightenment there to guide me in my predicament. I followed the path gestured to me and arrived at a Catholic church completely enclosed by a padlocked chain link fence. Arriving for 8:00 a.m. Mass, a priest unlocked a gate and a handful of us followed him inside.

What led to me being physically and emotionally adrift in a blighted neighborhood of New York City in the summer of 1981? While at ABC House earlier that year I had decided to take the summer off from camp, a sure sign of me needing to step back for a moment before deciding whether I wanted to continue moving forward on the same path. The previous summer I had stepped out of the camp director role to focus on the design of a new centralized nature program and a challenge program incorporating a ropes course. I was joined by a strong cast of Yawgoog staff in this effort, including my old tentmate Kent Harrop, as well as Billy Newman and Al Fenner. To help prepare for my new role I went to an educator program at North Carolina Outward Bound School during the April school vacation. There I encountered one of the earliest versions of a high ropes course. "High" was an apt descriptor, with the course located in some towering trees atop a mountain abutting the Pisgah National Forest on the outskirts of Asheville. While crossing "the beam" about seventy feet above the ground, I also encountered what climbers refer to as "sewing machine leg." I stared at my right leg dumbly as it started going up and down, really concerned about whether I could get it under control. I did, eventually. Not discouraged, and wanting to explore more the idea of working in outdoor adventure education, I decided to go back for a longer leadership program a year later. I felt ready to give up a summer at camp, with uncertainty about whether I would return. I had been traveling all night from North Carolina when the Datsun called for a timeout.

Seth and Irma saved me in the short term. I stayed at Seth's parents' home for a couple of nights in White Plains until the car was ready. But my longer-term path was unclear. The car had broken down, and I was close behind in my need for restoration. I limped home to my parents' house, drained. Struggling to get back up on my feet, and sorry for the summer timing, I let New Canaan know that I would not be returning to teach.

Feeling worn out, feeling the loss of a familiar sense of drive, and feeling my own vulnerability was unsettling and confusing. I felt estranged from myself and the here-and-now. I wasn't sure whether I simply needed a good respite or fundamentally a fresh direction. I was content for a while to float rather than swim, hoping that some watery path would emerge or some lighthouse beacon would appear to guide me.

But my time for reflection and renewal struggled with the sudden absence of structured activity and responsibility, not to mention a sense of purpose and direction. Morning runs, spending some time with Hoppy, and Monday night hoop with the newly married John Carty and friends at the Rhode Island School for the Deaf helped return some degree of equilibrium. I delved more deeply into Merton and attended a meeting for men thinking about the priesthood. I wrote a short piece for the *Providence Visitor*, the local diocesan newspaper, on the spiritual dimension of running, which I likened to the process of emptying oneself of superficial and more ego-centered concerns—"As the end of the run nears . . . I am stripped of non-essentials, closer to the bare and real me . . . I glimpse my honest, undecorated self." The *Visitor* also published my poem crying for more attention to the threat of nuclear holocaust. I ached to experience myself whole.

I roused myself to take a couple of courses at Providence College. One course was on moral problems taught by a Dominican priest with the disciplined mind of one of the order's forebears, Thomas Aquinas, which he applied unapologetically in scrutinizing my written work. He was not didactic; he wanted you to think. Among other things, the course forced me to consider important topics such as moral guidelines for the growing fields of biotechnology and genetic engineering, of moral means as well as moral ends when it comes to human ingenuity and the sacredness of human life. Some of the questions are still with me, including the question of how moral consciousness develops within and outside Catholic and Christian frames of reference, and how our collective moral consciousness responds and changes in the face of rapid technological advances.

The other course was on the classics of medieval Christian mystics, taught by an elderly Dominican nun with an ethereal presence that lent a translucent quality to her person and her words. There were only a few of us in her class, but she wasn't fazed in the least—it was the mystics who animated her. In her class I left questions of moral consciousness behind to encounter spiritual consciousness; shifted focus from understanding formed by theology and reasoning to understanding born from inner experience and to some extent religious imagining.

She introduced us to some of the most intriguing interior explorers of God's presence and love in the Christian tradition: *The Cloud of Unknowing*, Thomas à Kempis, Teresa of Avila, Catherine of Siena, and John of the Cross and his *Dark Night of the Soul.* I was taken especially by Juliana of Norwich and her *Revelations of Divine Love.* Juliana was an "anchoress," meaning she lived in solitude, devoting her life to contemplation, but also attached (anchored) to a place, in her case a church. Juliana's small room in the church had a window connecting her to the outside world. She developed a reputation for wise counsel and people sought her out. Her book is most of all an effort to assure us of the love and care of God for us—"All shall be well." Her unquestioned faith and account of her revelations seemed to me sometimes quaint, sometimes strange. But if I listened for the experience underlying her words, I could hear something real and deeply human, even relatable. She seemed intent on freeing minds and souls from undue worry, and her message seemed so unaffected, so sensitive to human yearning, and so much from the center of her being—assuring her readers that God "is the ground of our whole life in love"— it gave me heart. My daughter's name is Juliana, and she gives me heart, too.

Though engaged and enlightened by these excursions into moral and spiritual matters, I became increasingly aware that I could only float for so long pondering the waters of life and its depths. I was tipping well past the point of diminishing return; I greatly valued moments for reflection, recentering, and contemplation but felt that I needed to harness myself to a concrete social purpose and learn to integrate those moments into my active life. If a watery path wasn't going to appear like some grand revelation, then I would have to swim and make it myself.

And this is what I was learning to accept: that although I might not know exactly where I was going, there was a beacon to light my way regardless. A little brighter thanks to Juliana of Norwich, that beacon was a kind of reassurance that the current of joy coursing in me, however muted at times, was real, and that my effort to give myself genuinely and fully in whatever I was doing mattered. Midway through his life in the monastery, Merton had written a powerful prayer to express a similar idea:

> My Lord God, I have no idea where I am going. I do not see the road ahead of me. . . . Nor do I really know myself, and the fact that I think I am following your will does not mean that I am actually doing so. But I believe that the desire to please you does in fact please you. And I hope I have that desire in all that I am doing.

While I did not usually think in terms of following God's will, I found Merton's expression of desire and hope to be what God wanted him to be deeply familiar and moving, and I wanted to act with a similar integrity. I understood on some level that my effort to do so might itself be the most important path I was seeking; in other words, learning to live fully who I am would help me in whatever I chose to do. Merton again was enormously helpful. As he put it late in his monastic life, in his essay "Learning to Live": "And whatever you do, every act, however small, can teach you everything—provided you see who it is that is acting."

MAKING A PATH THROUGH WATER

During my watery wandering I spent a few days at Western Priory, a Benedictine monastery in Vermont located in a farm-like setting and, thanks in large part to Brother Gregory Norbet, noted for producing moving liturgical music. In keeping with the rule of St. Benedict, the monastic day combined periods of personal and communal prayer with study and work. Work might vary from mundane to skilled, artistic, or artisanal. Appropriately, I was assigned the mundane task of filling in the ruts in an unpaved roadway. I worked alongside a monk in plain work clothes. This monk turned out to be the abbot, or fatherly head, of the monastery. I was surprised for a moment; but then the full significance of his role struck me. He was at once a humble fellow monk and a pastoral leader and administrator; he was simply a member of the community who contributed to it according to his personal gifts and capabilities. That he was working with me literally to move some earth had added significance, because both humble and human have a common root in the Latin word "humus," meaning of the earth or ground. It was one of those moments, upon reflection, that seemed utterly simple and utterly profound. It highlighted for me how humility is not simply an isolated virtue on a checklist designed for the development of moral character, but also a matter of how we stand and act in our shared humanity, in the common ground of community.

By this time, I had moved far beyond thinking of morality in the binary terms of my childhood. Morality had a spiritual underpinning. That underpinning could be expressed in terms of relationship and community as fundamental and normal for human life. Thinking of relationship and community as a manifestation of a deeper spiritual unity helped, too.

My reading of the mystics and of Merton guided me in this respect, but I was learning also from others who thought similarly, such as Martin Luther King Jr. King understood nonviolent resistance as a force of love against injustice, not against people. Nonviolence was a spiritual not a physical force; it was a means to awaken the moral sense in others, the moral sense in all of us, so that we might better recognize injustice. Merton delved deeply into this idea in essays such as "Blessed are the Meek." He contrasts nonviolent resistance with efforts to assert or impose a righteous view or to control others, stressing instead the importance of trying to "awaken response" and engender an openness to dialogue "in which reason and love have freedom of action." For King, nonviolence was the path to actualizing what he referred to as the "beloved community." In keeping with his Christian faith tradition, we are all members of a beloved community, even if we do not all recognize it. It is up to us to open the space for that love to glimmer forth and grow in us.

As openness to love grows, the idea of justice opens also. Justice rooted in love searches for paths of equity and growth and not simply retribution. King, for example, sought to advance economic justice not only for its inherent importance in our social compact, in our commitment to opportunity for all, but also because it was important in bringing the beloved community to life. In forming their communities of growth and learning, many schools today practice "restorative justice"—a path for students, as well as adults, to express remorse and make concrete amends for an injury to one or more members of the community. It is a practice that reaffirms the dignity of each person while at the same time healing and renewing the community as a whole.

By this time I also had solidified other understandings that I felt worthy of my deep attention, although I admit they slipped in and out of my consciousness. These understandings were mostly in the form of pitfalls to avoid and fallacies of thinking parallel to Aristotle's fallacies of reasoning that Brother Stephen had introduced to us at La Salle. To codify a few of them:

- The fallacy of moral superiority and the authority to judge: how easy it is to fall into the trap of thinking we are better than others and judging accordingly. How easily we prance towards the precipice of the slippery slope of arrogance and omniscience—we all want to be gods! Or maybe we all need to assert the power of judgment simply because we don't have any other way to make ourselves feel strong and alive. Either way, I was caught on the precipice a few times, mainly by Dad during my youth.

  I learned that the desire to live "right," to take the moral high road, can slip into a self-approving sense of superiority. My father used to use the phrase "holier than thou" to refer to this kind of attitude; he could not abide pompousness. Once or twice (maybe three times) he might have applied the phrase to me in my adolescent years, together with the word "supercilious." Besides stimulating the vocabulary lobe in my brain, that initiated some needed introspection. I learned that the moment we think we are superior, we have proved that we are not.

  I remember shamefully when I wrote a letter to a district authority questioning the example set by Scout leaders of my troop. It's not that the standards I was upholding were wrong, but that my judgment was narrow and, frankly, smug; I chose to overlook the larger picture of their dedication.

  Even Christianity could work against itself. On the one hand, a moral virtue or teaching might be held up so high that it becomes a litmus test on whether one is righteous or not, worthy or not, a litmus test that can be wielded like a sword; on the other, teachings expressed in the Beatitudes, such as "Blessed are the poor in spirit" or "Blessed are the meek," encourage acting from humility and lovingkindness. If Christianity is about being like Christ or discovering Christ in yourself, then it is about learning to serve, live out of love and compassion, and be slow, very slow, to judge.

- The fallacy of perfection: Whether moral or intellectual or something else, the idea of perfection also can put you on a slippery slope towards self-delusion or frustration, or both. The pressure or delusion can also suck out the joy of life, not to mention, as Benjamin Franklin seemed all too aware, the life out of your relationships. My refrain to myself: instead of an ideal or delusional self, accept and embrace your real self, with all your internal pushes and pulls and blind spots, because perfection is a false god.
- The fallacy of false humility: This also is one of the fallacies that feed self-approval, or the desire for approval by others, more than the formation of your mature personhood. It can sometimes be hard to detect and sometimes the detection only comes with hindsight. Self-acceptance—learning to accept one's imperfection, to have self-empathy as well as empathy for others—is a good preventative.
- The pitfall of self-absorption: There is a fine line between self-reflection and self-absorption, and I crossed over from one to the other many times. I became aware of my tendency to dwell on things, partly from noticing others in my life who seemed to be able to shrug something off and move on more quickly than I did. I can think of many possible reasons for my own disposition, but ultimately what was important was to a) learn to recognize when I was in a self-absorbed rather than self-reflective state; b) consider joining brothers Rob and Joe in pointless yet entertaining and bonding banter to snap me out of it; c) do some aerobic activity like shooting hoops or a head-clearing run; and d) avoid ice cream as a palliative (avoiding was a tolerable standard, eliminating was an impossible one).
- Empathy, compassion, mercy, and justice are not mutually exclusive: the more we learn to treat each other as humans like ourselves, to act in empathy, the more likely we will act for wise justice (as compared to purely legalistic forms) and with regard for the well-being of each person and community. Empathy does not necessarily increase with age; but age is a sturdy friend in deepening it. If you pay even a modicum of attention to the vulnerabilities, fallibilities, and vagaries that come with being human, including your own, then you will activate the wisdom-granting power of aging.

My watery path was made up of ruminations such as these. I felt them deeply and they entered my consciousness, not for any specific or immediate purpose that I could ascertain, but to orient me in charting my course, and they still reside there for my consideration. At the same time, the question of what lay immediately ahead weighed heavily on me. To set my sights on solid ground, I took three concrete steps.

First, I recommitted to serving as camp director at Three Point at Yawgoog. I would continue in that role for four more summers, relishing the opportunity to work with a new generation of strong young leaders, some of whom I had known since they were young Scouts, many of whom decades later attended my seventieth birthday party. They included Tom Allen, gentle, full of integrity, and fond of ballads as well as the odd tale illustrating exceptional human endeavor, whom I recruited with a phone call during his university time abroad in Paris; Donnie Carlson, loyal scion of Troop 82 Providence, ready to serve, ready to convert an idea to action, and fully capable of generating and carrying out an idea if there wasn't one on hand; James Brayton Hall, flashing a perceptive sense of humor and a landscape designer even then, just turn him loose; Vinny Francisco, humble and ministerial; Mike Moniz, a born and conscientious adventurer, later to summit Mount Everest, among many other peaks; Howie Brightman, a true friend, a gifted celebrator of people and life, and unfettered explorer of possibility; Johnny Hopkins, Hop's youngest brother and irrepressibly vibrant and full of playful spirit; Greg Kelley, steward of all things operational; Shawn Donahue, whom we wrested away from political preoccupations in Providence to channel his thoughtful generosity into what we considered his true calling to support and guide alongside us; and Jeff Barnes, as reliable and trustworthy as you could hope.

Secondly, I applied to the Harvard doctoral program in education. I was motivated partly by my need for a more structured space to think and learn and partly by knowing Seth was applying, too. Harvard felt close enough geographically to keep me in touch with camp and Rhode Island; if I wasn't accepted, then I would probably return to teaching. My application essay began with a reference to Merton's "Learning to Live," a way to both introduce myself and signal the fundamental questions I hoped to address.

Finally, I jumped in midstream to teach English and religion at the all-girls St. Patrick's High School that my sister Kathy had attended for a short time. For the class on "Business English" (I didn't initially know what that meant, but it came with the job) I wish I could say that I did something creative and wonderful, such as simulating the activities of several different businesses; and that the girls representing these quasi-realistic businesses then started a series of interactions, like dominoes falling, that immersed them happily into the use of conventional writing tools such as memoranda and formal letters. But instead, I resorted to a dull and dreary textbook-and-skills-based approach—a C+ effort at best. With another group I spent overlong on a close reading of a young adult novel titled *Mrs. Mike*—one of the few with multiple copies in the school—at the expense of more Shakespeare. But the girls were responsible and eager and made the most of it, and I was grateful to be their teacher.

LUMINARIES, INFLUENCERS, AND MENTORS

After serving in June as Hop's best man at his wedding with Joan and another summer at camp, in the fall of 1982 I moved to Somerville in Massachusetts to live with Seth and Irma and began the last leg of my formal education at Harvard. There was plenty I could and would learn to help me understand better the complexities of education that I encountered head-on at ABC House and possibilities for helping all students thrive in the classroom. My secret hope was to finally knit together my trio of interests, also my three main realms of learning—teaching and learning in schools, the educational experience that had supported personal growth and a spirit of community at Yawgoog, and the inner experience and meaning-of-life questions represented by Merton—into my own Grand Unified Theory, my personal GUT. I didn't quite accomplish that, but I came surprisingly close. Just as important, as the poet Rainer Maria Rilke advised, I was trying better to live with the question of how to convert my interests and thinking into a personal direction—I suppose the question of my vocation and fulfillment as a person—because "the point is, to live everything." I understood that otherwise I would live in a constant state of contingency rather than in the embrace of the full experience of being me, including my uncertainties; that I would be living in the paradox of being blind to the gift and joy of life that Brother James at La Salle hoped we would all come to see and understand because I was too busy searching for it.

Focused on teaching and learning environments, but also wanting to understand education from multiple perspectives, including the spiritual perspective of Merton and the perspective of experiential education represented by Yawgoog, I took a wholistic approach in constructing my program of study. Where I had choices, I took courses that I saw as complementary parts of a whole rather than hone a specialization; I felt that I could not work exclusively on a single part if I didn't understand the whole. Coursework plunged me into ideas about teaching and learning and schooling, into clinical as well as systemic practices, into questions of human development and research, and yes, thanks to the Harvard Divinity School, which was a short walk from education classes on Appian Way through Cambridge Common and the grounds of the law school, into questions regarding spiritual experience. I also managed to set up an internship for academic credit at Project Adventure up the road in Hamilton.

As part of our extracurricular activity, Seth and I were awarded a grant from the Massachusetts state department of education to bring together about two dozen students from Belmont, a privileged largely white community, and the multiethnic, multiracial Fenway School in Boston, which was a new small "school-within-a-school" located atop the tall, narrow, and police-patrolled building housing English High School. Our hope was to exchange and explore perceptions of race and culture and community. We spent two weekends together at Yawgoog focused on relationship-building and communication and addressing these challenging topics. Our program carried its share of social and emotional risk; but we had willing participants, and the students and their teachers seemed to value the effort to break through stereotypes, with some resolving to become ambassadors of greater social awareness in their respective communities. The German chocolate cake with the girth and heft of a large tractor wheel was a hit, too, at our final get-together.

Ultimately, my experience at Harvard was more a matter of "who" than "what." Among the most prominent, there was Sara Lawrence Lightfoot, so elegant and powerful as a speaker and in her bearing, so observant and perceptive, and the first African American woman to receive tenure at the graduate school of education. I took two of her courses and was a teaching assistant for the one on the sociology of school systems, presumably asked to serve in this role on the strength of my paper on equality and education. But I discovered that I was not as qualified or experienced as the role needed; I learned much more than I contributed, including in my periodic meetings with Sara to discuss student experience in the course, during which I was so intent on listening that I forgot that I was in the role altogether. Carol Gilligan illuminated ideas regarding adolescent development by weaving literary passages with profound human texture and insight through her lectures, lighting up my humanities-educated brain. My advisor Don Oliver, also Seth's advisor, was exceptionally tolerant of divergent and exploratory thinking, not least because he engaged in it so liberally himself while pursuing his expansive interests in curriculum and cosmologies; I was lucky in this regard, since it was only fair that Don support my interest in Merton. Thanks to Irma acting on my behalf, I was guided at the Divinity School by Krister Stendahl, the former dean, in reading spiritual classics; he listened patiently to my meandering thought regarding people like St. Augustine and Martin Buber. With Karen, a petite and thoughtful Divinity School student whom I met in a course in education, I also took the course on spirituality offered by Henri Nouwen; I was drawn to it especially because I knew that Nouwen was influenced by Merton. Nouwen was a well-known priest and writer full of overflowing passion for a life-affirming spirituality, with compelling insight; but also with an approach that, sadly, he and others seemed to have difficulty reconciling with an academic environment intent on using critical lenses such as social structure and power and feminism to examine religious tradition and practice. Only decades later did my Yawgoog friend Kent and I discover that we had both taken this course; Kent, staying true to the vocational calling that he shared with me in our tent at camp, while studying for the ministry at Andover Theological Seminary.

Several of my close Yawgoog friends were in the vicinity at various points of my Harvard years. Howie Brightman and Tom Allen, whom I've already introduced, were at Tufts University, a short walk from where I lived in Somerville and from one of our important rendezvous points—the new and wildly popular Steve's Ice Cream, replete with various homemade flavors and a plethora of tasty optional toppings. Julio Friedmann, a younger member of our staff with an endearing propensity for absent-minded pauses and faraway looks suggesting deep engagement with invisible parts of the universe, was beginning at MIT, a prelude to a career focused on energy and world-class expertise in subjects such as carbon capture and CO_2 removal. Donnie Carlson was at Harvard Law. We bolstered our spirits by gathering occasionally at Pizzeria Uno in Harvard Square for lunch, Julio often pulling out a bag of change, mostly pennies, to contribute his share. Donnie was taking a course titled "Dickens and the Law" taught by polymath humanitarian Robert Coles. He introduced me to "Bob" one day after his class and Bob, a student of the moral and spiritual lives of children and adults and as busy as anyone at Harvard, after listening to my awkward attempt to explain what I was doing, right on the spot signed on to be one of my dissertation readers. It was a propitious moment, Yawgoog, my personal interests, and my academic work somehow tying together.

Of all the figures in the story of my learning at Harvard, three were especially compelling, although, ironically, only one actually taught there. They were Eleanor Duckworth, author of the course on "Teaching and Learning;" Karl Rohnke, adventure education guru; and of course, Merton. Just as I always had a book ready to read in my desk in elementary school, I always carried a Merton volume in my backpack. His *New Seeds of Contemplation* and essays compiled in *Love and Living* were favorites, mainly because I felt they easily withstood multiple and meditative re-readings; there was so much contained in almost every word.

ELEANOR AND THE POWER OF OUR MINDS

No course intrigued me more than "Teaching and Learning." I had encountered many of the intricacies and opacities of both as a teacher—here was a chance for illumination.

I'm not sure how I expected illumination to be delivered, but I quickly learned with my peers that it wouldn't be in the form of a sacred text or a single epiphany. Eleanor Duckworth, the professor, gave us one main directive: to pay attention to our own thoughts and their evolution as well as to the thoughts of others and their evolution as we considered one thing or another. We were being asked to learn anew about learning by becoming closely observant learners ourselves.

Eleanor had been a protégé of Jean Piaget, whose theory of cognitive development charted a new direction in the field. Broadly speaking, Piaget was a student of how we come to know what we know. From Piaget's effort to learn what and how children were thinking, Eleanor distilled an important idea about teaching and learning: provide some interesting and meaningful subject matter, then work carefully to make sense of the sense the learners are making in the engagement that follows; use what you learn, together with your knowledge of possible byways and pathways of learning the subject matter, to figure out how the learners might move *themselves* to greater understanding. And why do this? Because, to use Eleanor's lovely and evocative phrase, captured in a book with the same title, "the having of wonderful ideas"—that is, ideas that we hatch all on our own, that are new to us even if they may have occurred already to others—ignites the power of our minds.

I was as guilty as any other teacher (or parent or friend) in wanting students to figure out something for themselves, only to insert hints, exaggerated winks, verbal nudges, and outright answers into *their* process, thus diluting the opportunity for them to experience the power of their own minds. Eleanor's directive in the course to learn to pay attention to our own thinking and the thinking of others was meant to slow down hasty teaching reflexes and replace them with carefully considered responses calculated to keep the learner moving along their path of learning.

To give one example of the learning experiences we had with Eleanor, I'll take you on a short encounter with the moon. Before the course, my encounters with the moon were sporadic, fleeting, and mostly incidental. I had some aesthetic appreciation for the graceful and sometimes mysterious and spectral presence of our smaller sibling sphere, but little knowledge of it. Not that I was wholly uninterested and detached; as I mention in the first pages of this narrative, I was enthralled with the Apollo 11 landing as a kid, watching in awe as Neil Armstrong gingerly made the first human imprint on the surface. I scrutinized a lunar rock when the national tour of an Apollo capsule made it to Providence. I earned astronomy merit badge, which required some moon study. But did I have a wondering or inquiring relationship with the moon? Did I understand the moon and what Eleanor referred to as "its habits"? Could I tell you where it would be and what it would look like from one night to the next from my lunar observation post? Could I tell you why it would be where it would be and look like it did? Sadly, no. On a scale of "understanding the moon" that starts with "lives like a mole" and ends with Galileo, I would be with all those living underground.

My lunar education really began in Eleanor's class. I sketched the location and shape of the moon from my observation post when the night sky was clear, usually at the same time in the evening as Eleanor advised, so that I could easily compare one night to the next. I listened to the observations of my classmates when we shared our moon data. Sometimes this felt like a laborious process, as we noted what we saw, the changes in size and shape, the unexpected changes, and frustrations with light pollution or the unexplainable disappearances of the moon. We were discouraged from theorizing or introducing any formalized bits of knowledge during our sharing—although some of us tried, calling on memories of paper mache models of the earth, moon, and solar system in elementary school or images from a textbook. Some science teachers especially struggled with this restriction; they wanted to share what they knew.

But there is a fundamentally different kind of knowing at work when you must look up at the sky and begin to make sense of what you see; when you have to make your way through the fogginess of not knowing, as if you're an ancient mariner searching for glimmers of light or landmarks, or sailing in uncharted waters, forming a map in your head as you go, maybe drawing the map as well; when you have to rely on patient persistent observation, wondering, and muddling through; when you're doing your best imitation of Galileo. And Eleanor wanted us to experience this kind of knowing. She wanted us to experience our capacity to shine a light on complexity. She wanted to remind us of what it takes to journey from the unknown to understanding, the journeys classroom learners are asked to take every day. So intent was she, that she far surpassed us in her patience and close attentiveness to our observations and questions. In moments of thoughtful pause, she sometimes formed with us a way we might go about answering a question or work through a confusion one or more of us tried to articulate. She insisted by her example, and occasionally by an admonishing look or word, that we be and do the same; that we become a learning community.

For me, the idea of trying to notice the habits of the moon, to treat the moon as a natural phenomenon with its own set of behaviors, made it feel less distant, more connected. I was recording observations, but in a larger sense I was building a relationship, getting to know a part of our world better.

I got to the point where I could predict what the moon would look like during a given monthly period, one day to the next; when it would be growing towards a "full" circular size or waning to a thumbnail-shaped sliver before slipping from view; where I might see it and when I might not. But then I noticed that the location seemed to change from one month to the next—one month's data wouldn't predict the next one's, not exactly. I realized that my evolving mental map of the moon's behavior had to account for how perspective changed from one season to the next, too. Some of my classmates noted changes in brightness and hue. And what about the question of a lunar eclipse? What about connecting the habits of the moon to the behavior of nearby ocean tides? How would you calculate where the moon would be if you were planning a lunar landing?! As a curriculum the moon is rich in texture and complexity. Figure out one thing and then the fog rolls in again. But moments of clarity are contagious—have one and you just might want to go sailing for another, with increased confidence and stamina. Indeed, I continued my learning with Eleanor in "Teaching and Learning" as well as in a course on understanding school practice for several years as a teaching fellow. Decades later, my lunar education continues, haphazardly I must admit. Eleanor has studied the moon steadily all this time, often with friends.

My admiration for Eleanor's particularity in attending to the thinking of others, for the meticulous care in her effort to clarify and understand, only grew during my several years learning with her. To be a teacher in the mold of Eleanor meant to engage the interest and ideas of your students; meant being an observer, a learner, and an inquirer into their thoughts; meant to exclaim with them at moments of insight and wonder. Even more, I came to realize how much Eleanor's attentiveness was more than a clinical exercise, how it reflected Eleanor's conviction that all can learn; how it reflected her deep respect not only for a mind at work, but also for the person whose mind is working; how inviolable Eleanor regarded the process of each person's own coming-to-know. She is with them finding ways to support them on *their* journey.

Eleanor in this way reinforced for me the deeply human nature of education. To be with another on their journey of learning is a profound affirmation—of them but also of ourselves. Learning matters and they matter. The journey of their learning is entirely personal, but it also is a personal version of the larger journey we all share. Whether as teacher or parent or friend, being with them is an act of empathy and solidarity.

KARL AND THE ART OF ADVENTURE LEARNING

While taking Eleanor's course on teaching and learning, I began spending one day a week at Project Adventure. Project Adventure was the epicenter of adventure programming and for me an adventure nursery; for it was there that ropes course elements and teamwork-building initiatives were being born. And the chief innovator was Karl Rohnke. Karl was the author of *Cowstails and Cobras*, the ropes course and adventure programming bible that I had consulted in my work at camp.

Karl's journey to Project Adventure included a stint at Outward Bound in North Carolina, where he was an instructor from 1969-1971, a decade before I attended programs there. Karl was an athlete, outdoorsman, and serious competitor, having captained the track and field, soccer, and swimming teams at Washington and Lee University at different times. He thrived on challenge. And so did the North Carolina Outward Bound School, inspired by the words of Kurt Hahn to cultivate "an enterprising curiosity; an undefeatable spirit; tenacity in pursuit; readiness for sensible self-denial; and, above all, compassion." Karl was party to one of the more grueling tasks posed by the Outward Bound staff—carrying a backpack weighted with rocks on a steep climb up Table Rock Mountain. What could be better?!

Plenty, as it turns out. Physical challenge was one way to discover your capacities but was limited by its traditional cast in a military or competitive sports mold. The more fundamental questions were how we greet and meet any challenge, how any of us surpasses the limits we consciously or unconsciously set for ourselves. When do we venture beyond our self-perceived capabilities and discover something new about who we are and what we can do? In close tandem, what conditions and contexts support our trying? And how does this learning occur in different groups? These were educational questions, and a world of possibility opens in trying to answer them.

Karl never lost his competitive spirit. Often he channeled it into physical goals he set for himself, such as doing ten thousand pull-ups (palms outward) to invigorate down time during winter. As he aged, he competed in masters swimming events and eventually the Senior Olympics, confiding at one point that his chances of winning were good since he likely would be the only competitor in his event (the fifty meter butterfly). But his greatest feat might have been his leap from competitor to educator. He became absorbed by the question of how to engage others in an experience of doing something they didn't know they could do, of how to help them reap the benefits to mind and spirit that flow from accomplishing something perceived as challenging. If being with Eleanor was a case study in tapping the human capacity to have wonderful ideas, being with Karl was a tutorial in how to construct challenges as satisfying experiences in self-discovery. Sometimes you literally had to stretch and hang on to get the full experience, as I learned when Karl asked me to help him build his new climbing wall.

Whether we ease in or jump in, challenges must stretch us for learning to happen. Sometimes the stretching is very real, as it was when I found myself spread-eagled on a windowless red brick facade of the multistory

Project Adventure building, formerly a schoolhouse. Like a lot of what Karl did, the climbing wall did not have a blueprint; indeed, if you used the term climbing wall in spring of 1983, most people would imagine a cliff face carved by geological power, like Half-Dome in Yosemite. Project Adventure's first climbing wall would be an organic process.

Karl had played around with different kinds of handholds and footholds and how to attach them; but plotting out a climbing route was a different matter. Six feet, three inches tall, Karl had the wingspan of a condor, against which I looked like a mere nestling. When he looked at me and the wall, he saw a measuring rod.

How to begin? Like any good learning curriculum, the first move on the wall had to invite interest and balance accessibility and challenge. Karl affixed the first block experimentally. I would try to grasp it, throw out my right leg to hook my foot on a protruding rough edge of concrete, and boost myself; it was an exercise in maneuvering horizontally and finding leverage. As I recall, we moved the block to adjust to my efforts a couple of times but more often I had to adjust to the block.

After we figured out the starting point, the next phase of the building process entailed putting me on belay—in this case, harnessing me to a safety rope that looped through some carabiners connected to nylon webbing that encircled an anchoring chimney on the roof and wrapped partially around Karl standing on the ground. I would then stretch in one direction or another while hoping to maintain a tenuous foothold. Karl would consider the angle and distance of my reach as I hung on, then lower me down and, while I belayed, put a new block or two in the general vicinity of where my fingers or toes had just been. Karl's placement reflected a generous view of my elasticity and stretchability; in a very vivid way, he was constructing the learning space between what I could do and what I could potentially do with support—what the educational theorist Lev Vygotsky termed "the zone of proximal development."

As Karl seemed to have a good impression of me, I wanted to measure up. For his part, I think Karl had confidence in my ability to figure out that I could do more than I might perceive; that my reach, in the words of the poet Robert Browning, could exceed my grasp. And he trusted that I would find that faith in myself. Faith and trust were the mainstay of his support through Vygotsky's learning zone.

There was a certain irony in my wall learning with Karl. Like much learning, it entailed a lot of letting go, together with some courage in the face of uncertainty, as well as trust and attentiveness. Letting go of my desire to prove to Karl what I could do. Letting go of the fear of failure. Stubbornly confronting uncertainty with possibility. The trust included my trust in Karl as my belayer—I was never worried about falling. But I also needed to trust in my own learning. Furthermore, I needed to trust in Karl's patient support of my learning without judgment, a quality of Karl as educator that I quickly grew to admire and appreciate. With climbing these fundamental elements of learning are heightened significantly; to varying degrees we are more aware of them, and our awareness can get in the way.

Karl became adept at helping people get out of their own way. He appropriated the unfamiliar as well as the allure of play as learning tools—creating situations outside the realm of experience of most people, neutralizing advantages of skill that some might have while kindling curiosity as well as the perception of challenge. To some extent, he contrived to lure them in, let their engagement morph into absorption, and let absorption take its natural course, with due attention to ensuring a safe emotional and physical environment. Emblematic, one of Karl's signature get-to-know-you activities involved a group in a broad circle tossing a soft squeezable ball one to another while calling out each other's name. Throwing and catching start slowly, punctuated with tentative salutations and thank-yous. The tactile experience changes when a fuzzy ball appears. The pace quickens as balls multiply along with the number of errant tosses, until a rubber chicken joins the exchange and the name-calling cacophony erupts in breathless guffaws. Karl never saw a need to process activities like this one. He respected exhilaration as a powerful teacher.

During my internship Karl guided a group in a rappelling experience of the face-first variety—a rappel that faces you downward rather than to the sky is a compelling reminder of gravity as one of the fundamental forces in the universe, and I presumed that learning to thrive with this reminder was the main point of it. When the group departed, Karl and I eased our backsides onto a slab of granite atop the rappelling hill and ate our homemade lunches. I learned that Karl kept a notebook of quotations he found meaningful, both humorous and serious, just as I did. We exchanged a couple of our favorite insights, discovering something of the vistas within each of us. We would trade insights now and then—of course in a verbally playful way (Karl was adroit in this regard, too, even in what he once termed his "caducity," a word I had to look up)—for most of the rest of his life.

Karl was tantamount to a spiritual master in his field. Like all true spiritual masters, he didn't make himself the center of learning but instead worked to center the learner in an experience planted with seeds of self-discovery. At his invitation I once joined the final activity of an adventure education class he taught at Boston University, which entailed climbing one of the light towers rimming a sports field bordered on one side by the Massachusetts turnpike, with Karl perched on top in the light tower cage. The last one up, as I poked my head into the narrow cage opening, Karl greeted me in a meditative pose, eyes twinkling, unable to suppress a smile, and asked, "What do you seek?!"

Karl followed his creative adventuring muse. He took the road that was true to himself, the one that made him whole; the road that is uniquely ours to discover and follow. And he reassured me—perhaps better, helped me reassure myself—that I was on that road, too, not necessarily in terms of adventure education, but simply in being the person I was.

THOMAS MERTON AND LEARNING TO BE WHAT WE ARE

In their different ways, both Eleanor and Karl affirmed people as they are, affirmed them as persons full of wonderful capacities they might not fully apprehend or know how to activate. I experienced this fundamental affirmation in my family, in Sr. Theresa giving me her folder of articles on U.S. presidents in fourth grade, in Brother James's classes at La Salle, and at every stage of my staff life at Camp Yawgoog. It is the starting point for all true education; that is, education in its root meaning, derived from Latin words denoting "bringing up" or "nourishing," as well as "leading out" and "bringing forth." Education in this sense means affirming and bringing forth all that we are, not only for ourselves but also for others.

Thomas Merton also considered education a process of discovering what we are and forming ourselves as whole persons. There was a distinctively monastic cast to Merton's understanding—for him the monastery was a place dedicated to the realization of your authentic self in God. As he explained to his fellow monks, this did not mean that you were trying to live up to some spiritual ideal. Discovering yourself in God meant learning to be fully yourself, to be you.

As much outside as inside the monastic enclosure, learning to be yourself entailed learning to let go of what Merton characterized as "the false drive for self-affirmation." Merton considered us susceptible especially to affirmation dependent on the various messages of success or approval or failure in society, messages, as he knew, that were proliferating with the expansion of media influence well underway in his time. Get caught up in a social world that encourages the false drive for self-affirmation and you're feeding what Merton described variously as a "false" or "superficial" or "external" self. Strive instead for authenticity in the ordinary process of learning about yourself in and through others, in your social and cultural life. Consider also opening yourself to greater awareness of your whole being.

For Merton, we are already affirmed in our whole being in the love of God. Our full authentic self is not an identity we construct or that is constructed for us but rather the very self we are, affirmed in love. Our experience of human affirmation—in family, in our closest social groups, in friendship, in educational experiences of the quality and depth represented by educators like Eleanor and Karl—is not only inherently important, but also an intimation of love that embraces us whole.

Merton makes clear that the love animating our very being is not only personal but also mutual. You and I are more than interconnected and interdependent individuals in an ecological or economic sense. Beyond even our common genetic heritage, the common atomic elements of our physical selves, and our shared cultural lives, we are deeply related, and awareness of our relatedness helps us to be what we are. As he wrote in response to a "Merton evening" held at Smith College in Massachusetts, we are all one in "that hidden ground of love for which there can be no explanations." In kinship with the idea of "human" as grounded in the earth, with Juliana of Norwich's assurance of God as "the ground of our whole life in love," and with King's concept of the "beloved community," the hidden ground of love is the sustaining source of our lives as persons and as members of the human community. Our common vocation as humans is to learn together to live in it.

Merton expressed his experience of the hidden ground of love in a burst of exuberance in a well-known passage from *Conjectures of a Guilty Bystander*, one of his journals that he edited for publication (I have a framed poster of it). The passage describes a moment of epiphany he had while on a rare visit to Louisville, Kentucky, about an hour north of his monastery. It marks a pivotal turn in his monastic journey that started with withdrawal from the world only to return him with a radical awareness of his shared humanity. Watching the people of the city as he stood at the corner of what today is Fourth and Muhammad Ali, Merton writes:

> . . . I was suddenly overwhelmed with the realization that I loved all those people, that they were mine and I theirs, that we could not be alien to one another even though we were total strangers. It was like waking from a dream of separateness . . . I have the immense joy of being [human], a member of a race in which God Himself became incarnate. . . . And if only everybody could realize this! . . . There is no way of telling people that they are all walking around shining like the sun.

Fully restored as a member of the human community, in the 1960s Merton became one of its most discerning and vocal members. At the same time that he followed the personal and communal life of prayer of his monastery, and even as he lived for the last few years of his life in a hermitage on his monastery's grounds, he grew to commune in a real sense with the world at large, connecting through his correspondence, and on occasion in person at the hermitage, with poets, religious figures, nonviolent, anti-war, and social justice activists, and young people, among others. In his hermitage he played the Beatles and Joan Baez's Silver Dagger album. He stood up, stood with, and stood for a more humane and just world most of all through his social writing. He was responding in the 1960s to a world all too familiar to us in the twenty-first century—a world where threats of nuclear destruction still occur, a world burdened by racial strife, poverty, inequity, and war, a world in need of greater interreligious, intercultural, cross-cultural, and ecological understanding.

And this is what happens when you orient yourself to a deeper affirmation, a deeper relatedness to others, to the "immense joy of being human" in "the hidden ground of love": you feel the importance of learning, in your unique personal way in your niche in the world, how you can stand up, stand with, and stand for. Merton in this regard was a teacher as well as writer. He offered valuable perspective and guidance, especially to activists eager to make a difference in the name of peace and justice.

Merton conveyed one of his most compelling messages in a letter to James Forest, a young advocate for peace in the face of the Vietnam war. Forest was part of a group that Merton gathered in 1964 for a retreat at his hermitage to explore "the spiritual roots of protest." In 1966 an overwhelmed Forest writes to Merton with a sense of impotence and disillusionment: "I feel like an ant climbing a cliff, and even worse, for in the distance there seems to be an avalanche . . . Perhaps you have some thoughts that would help?"

In a considered response, Merton counsels Forest not to place his hope in visible results. Be wary, similarly, of how zeal for a "cause" can dominate your field of vision to the point of blinding you to what your work is truly about. We are susceptible to the pull of our own desire and need, believing in something so strongly that we cannot accept anything except the result foreordained in our minds, wanting it so strongly that we can confuse fulfilling our want, proving our own rightness, whether privately or publicly, for the real thing. This path is misleading because it is oriented to building an "identity" from our work; it centers the work on us more than we might realize. Merton emphasizes instead the importance of shifting attention from ideology to people. "Gradually," Merton tells Forest, "you struggle less and less for an idea and more and more for specific people. The range tends to narrow down, but it gets much more real." Merton suggests that when the focus is on people, there is a greater possibility for love to enter in and guide us: "All the good you do will not come from you but from the fact that you have allowed yourself . . . to be used by God's love."

In shifting attention from results to people, from righteous cause to action guided by love, Merton was reminding Forest of the "spiritual roots of protest" and indeed, the spiritual roots of any action on behalf of others or what we hope is for a greater good. How might we approach any work from our deepest identity as persons joined together in the hidden ground of love, from an effort to be fully "what we are"? Merton's person-centered and love-guided counsel seemed so relevant to me and almost everything I had done and would do. I had another pitfall to avoid, another seed of wisdom to try to nurture.

I started my Harvard journey with an application essay that drew from Merton's "Learning to Live." So it was fitting that I return to Merton to conclude my journey. After exploring a few different possibilities, including a focus on Camp Yawgoog as a culture for personal growth, I wrote my dissertation on Merton and education, an immersive experience that culminated in spring of 1987, just after I turned thirty-two years old. True to the genre of dissertation, it is basically an elaborate and much denser version of what I've written above. But sometimes you will see the forest better and more fully when you've spent some time getting to know the different trees as well as the intricate and interwoven features that lie below its canopy. My effort to get to know Merton in breadth and depth helped me to understand not just his life but also the development and broader significance of his Christian humanism, his contemplative way of seeing and knowing, his lived awareness of and compassionate response to our relatedness, and his freedom of being.

MY GRAND UNIFIED THEORY

I learned a tremendous amount during the last leg of my formal education—about education in theory and practice, yes; but more importantly about education as a process of affirming and enabling us to grow more fully into who we are, which means not for ourselves alone but as co-members of a democratic society and the larger human society and ecological world. To the extent that I formed a unified theory of education and life, it was at this nexus of formal intellectual learning, experiential adventure learning, and spiritual awareness.

I also felt more deeply the current of joy that has flowed in me since childhood, that was freer and stronger than any other but that I frequently forgot or neglected in my preoccupations; the same current reminding me of the gift and joy of being human that Brother James tried to help us discover, and of love that animates me as me and everyone else as who they are. I would try to do my best to live more mindful of it, more responsive to it. I would have much to learn and relearn about bringing myself, my understandings, and my experience together in facing challenges and complexities ahead. But if my personal compass could not tell me where to go, it would remind me who I am, how to be and why, and what matters along the way.

Providence was a generative force in my journey, and with all that it generated I can see it also as an inexplicable guiding force in the sense understood by Roger Williams. My family's life was born there. Providence made St. Mary's, La Salle, Brown, Rhode Island College, and Yawgoog possible. It was a Brown connection in the person of Cathy Clark that led me to New Canaan, one New Canaan connection, Steve at ABC House, that introduced me to Merton, and another in the persons of Seth and Irma that drew my attention to Harvard. My family and Providence gave me the community of my life, a community that lives in me. They all provided me with the opportunity to understand and grow and live being me and what we are.

5

Footprints at the Edge of the Sea

"... no one [can] write truthfully about the sea and leave out the poetry."

—Rachel Carson

Several times during the 1960s we spent a week or more at one of the small summer cottages facing Scarborough Beach on Desano Drive, transporting us into a different and seemingly carefree world suffused with the sounds of the shore—the waves with their rhythm of rushing sounds, the piercing calls of the seagulls, the foghorn with a deep roar like a strange animal—and the still salty air at night. The early mornings were dew-drenched and quiet, unencumbered by the people sounds that would arrive later.

By seven a.m. or so the young day was beckoning us out. Dad would gather Rob and I for a beachward jaunt while Mom got Kathy and Joey ready for the day. We would gather our beach blanket and towels and pails and swing into step. Dad sometimes would march us in military cadence—"Gotta get home on your left, your right! Sound off . . ."—heightening our sense of adventure. The early morning beach was pristine, the sand-grooming machine just finishing its work of turning over and furrowing the sand, with perhaps two or three early morning walkers in the distance. Usually, we would set up on the left side of the pavilion about three-fourths of the way down the stretch of sand leading to the attenuating and frothy waves.

Dad liked "riding the waves," and we would follow his example and try catching them just as they were about to break, doing our best to hold our bodies straight with arms outstretched in the swirl and tumult. Rob and I would soon get to work with our pails, scooping up sand, packing it in, and turning the pails over to create a sand pie in the shape of the pail. We might make dozens of these, stretched out like dragons' teeth or the crenellated walls of a castle. Then, when the spirit moved us, we would run helter-skelter to demolish them with our feet in rapid succession, animated by nothing more than the sheer delight of doing it.

I might sometimes try to judge the pace and distance a wave would travel before it reached my toes, sometimes running away at the last second, sometimes jumping forward to make a splash. I might also watch my footprints fill in with water and eventually disappear in the washing and smoothing action.

Those footprints grew over time, and each time they would make an imprint, and each time they would become full whether I saw it or not, and then slowly fade into the rhythmic life of the sand, the waves, the beach. They continued in this way, adding to their cumulative effect in time and place and people and memory and understanding.

Epilogue

AMAZING HOW THE LONG-AGO can suddenly seem present and real. I didn't realize how much of my journey was imprinted on me, how much part of my experience of being me, until I started to write it. And writing reminded me of many things, including how so many lives have impacted mine, how precious they are and life is, how deeply interwoven our lives are.

Hoppy and I lost all too soon John Carty ("the Pelican"), one of our closest Yawgoog friends, as well as Hop's brother John. Our adventures are fewer now, but no less enjoyable and nourishing for our spirits and our friendship born at Yawgoog. And we are both deeply grateful for the special women in our lives.

Elena, the perceptive woman who nudged me to host my seventieth birthday celebration, and I were among the early users of dating web sites, grateful to have technology in our busy lives to help us find each other. She grew up in Belarus as a citizen of the Soviet Union until its break-up in 1991. Elena and her wonderful children Natasha and Andrei joined Juliana and me to make our new family.

My daughter Juliana is a writer and active in film directing. Her mom, Karen, was my companion in Henri Nouwen's course on spirituality at Harvard. Although our marriage did not endure, Juliana is a bright light for both of us, and for me a partner in verbal play. She also is a partner in the word game Boggle, winning almost every time and by huge margins. But I play with her anyway, for the fun of finding an especially sinuous word and for the joy of basking in her prowess. She loved Paul Simon's sound from the moment I introduced it (a Simon song is my ringtone for her) and otherwise makes sure that I am kept abreast of contemporary music, film, and literary voices.

The ABC House in New Canaan is still going strong, still responding to the effects of systemic inequity, having graduated ninety-two scholars during its fifty-year history. Their web site lists several alumni scholars from my year there; one went to Columbia University, another to Wesleyan University, and another to Union College.

Merton died in 1968, well before Steve handed me his autobiography at ABC House. But I had several opportunities to visit Gethsemani Abbey (his monastery), as well as his hermitage, and to meet his secretary, Brother Patrick Hart, and other monks who knew him, including those who studied under his guidance as novices.

I was a member of the first group of students to take Eleanor's course; she continued for decades more. I was grateful for the opportunity to talk about my experience learning from her during a tribute when she retired and to help celebrate her ninetieth birthday while finishing this book.

Karl helped me add some elements to the ropes course at Yawgoog before camp opened for the summer in 1983, and we regularly traded notes on fitness and adventuring until his passing.

Seth continued as a dynamic educator at the University of Massachusetts in Amherst, focusing on education and social issues, until his sudden death at the age of thirty-three. Irma helped bring to fruition his book, *Transforming Power: Domination, Empowerment, and Education.*

My work in education unfolded in ways that I did not anticipate but that felt true to my vocational compass. It focused mainly on enhancing learning for future educators, practicing educators, and students through collaboration, partnership, and community-building. It took place in an underserved multilingual, multiethnic neighborhood full of wonderful kids living in two- and three-decker houses just like the ones of my childhood in Providence, kids who taught me and colleagues every day about powerful minds, hearts, and aspirations.

I follow the Celtics and Red Sox as fervently as ever, comparing notes with Rob and Joe regularly, with Juliana often, and sometimes with Kathy and Frank. I still go to Providence for pizza—it's the best in the world. I occasionally meet my siblings at Caserta's or Twins or Rosa Mia's, or for a lunch at Luigi's in Johnston; and it's not unusual to make a stop at Sal's Bakery on Chalkstone or Palmieri's for some fresh Italian bread or a spinach pie on the way home.

Bibliography

Adams, Henry. *The Education of Henry Adams*. Boston: Houghton Mifflin, 1918.

Baldwin, James. "A Talk to Teachers." In *The Graywolf Annual Five: Multicultural Literacy*, edited by R. Simonson and S. Walker, 3–12. Saint Paul: Graywolf, 1988.

Barry, John M. *Roger Williams and the Creation of the American Soul: Church, State, and the Birth of Liberty*. New York: Viking, 2012.

Brooks, Paul. *The House of Life: Rachel Carson at Work with Selections from Her Writings Published and Unpublished*. Boston: Houghton Mifflin, 1972.

Carson, Rachel. *The Sea Around Us*. New York: Oxford University Press, 1951.

———. *Silent Spring*. Boston: Houghton Mifflin, 1962.

Deetz, James. *Invitation to Archaeology*. New York: Natural History, 1967.

Del Prete, Thomas. *Thomas Merton and the Education of the Whole Person*. Birmingham: Religious Education, 1990.

———. "Thomas Merton's Spirituality of Education." *Catholic Education: A Journal of Inquiry and Practice* 5, no. 2 (2001) 157–180. https://doi.org/10.15365/joce.0502042013.

Dickinson, Emily. *Final Harvest: Emily Dickinson's Poems*. Boston: Little, Brown, 1961.

Donald, David Herbert. *Lincoln*. New York: Simon & Schuster, 1995.

Duckworth, Eleanor. *"The Having of Wonderful Ideas" and Other Essays on Teaching and Learning*. 3rd ed. New York: Teachers College, 2006.

Frankl, Viktor E. *Man's Search for Meaning: An Introduction to Logotherapy*. New York: Washington Square, 1963.

Franklin, Benjamin. *Benjamin Franklin: The Autobiography and Selections from His Other Writings*. Edited by L. Jesse Lemisch. New York: Signet, 1961.

Heschel, Abraham Joshua. *The Insecurity of Freedom: Essays on Human Existence*. New York: Schocken, 1972.

Juliana of Norwich. *Revelations of Divine Love*. Translated by M. L. Del Mastro. New York: Image, 1977.

King, Martin Luther Jr. *Stride Toward Freedom: The Montgomery Story*. San Francisco: Harper & Row, 1958.

Lincoln, Abraham. "Cooper Union Address." Abraham Lincoln Online, Speeches & Writings, Sept. 20, 2025. https://www.abrahamlincolnonline.org/lincoln/speeches/cooper.htm.

McPhee, John. *A Sense of Where You Are*. New York: Farrar, Straus, Giroux, 1965.

Merton, Thomas. *The Asian Journal of Thomas Merton*. Edited by Naomi Burton, Brother Patrick Hart, and James Laughlin. New York: New Directions, 1975.

———. *Conjectures of a Guilty Bystander*. New York: Doubleday, 1966.

———. *The Hidden Ground of Love: Letters*. Edited by William Shannon. New York: Farrar, Straus, Giroux, 1985.

———. *New Seeds of Contemplation*. New York: New Directions, 1961.

———. *The Nonviolent Alternative* (original edition published as *Thomas Merton on Peace*). Edited by Gordon C. Zahn. New York: Farrar, Straus, Giroux, 1980.

———. *The Seven Storey Mountain*. New York: Harcourt, Brace, Jovanovich, 1948.

———. *Thoughts in Solitude*. New York: Farrar, Straus and Giroux, 1958.

Rohnke, Karl. *Cowstails & Cobras: A Guide to Ropes Courses, Initiative Games, and Other Adventure Activities*. Dubuque: Kendall/Hunt, 1977.

———. *Silver Bullets: A Guide to Initiative Problems, Adventure Games, Stunts and Trust Activities*. Hamilton, MA: Project Adventure, 1984.

Sarton, May. "Now I Become Myself." All Poetry, Sept. 7, 2025. https://allpoetry.com/now-i-become-myself.

Silverman, David J. *This Land Is Their Land: The Wampanoag Indians, Plymouth Colony, and the Troubled History of Thanksgiving*. New York: Bloomsbury, 2019.

Williams, Roger. *A Key into the Language of America: Or, an Help to the Language of the Natives in that Part of America Called New-England*. London: Gregory Dexter, 1643.

Wood, Gordon S. *The Americanization of Benjamin Franklin*. New York: Penguin, 2004.

———. *The Creation of the American Republic, 1776-1787*. Chapel Hill: University of North Carolina, 1969.

www.ingramcontent.com/pod-product-compliance
Lightning Source LLC
LaVergne TN
LVHW020626100826
845148LV00012B/2071

* 9 7 9 8 3 8 5 2 7 1 3 5 1 *